a mystery
of majesty

a mystery
of majesty

An Intimate Look at
a Loving God

Dennis Jernigan

• THE ARTISTS DEVOTIONAL SERIES •

HOWARD
PUBLISHING CO.
West Monroe, Louisiana

Our purpose at Howard Publishing is to:

- *Increase faith* in the hearts of growing Christians
- *Inspire holiness* in the lives of believers
- *Instill hope* in the hearts of struggling people everywhere

Because He's coming again!

A Mystery of Majesty
© 1997 by Dennis Jernigan
All rights reserved. Printed in the United States of America

Published by Howard Publishing Co., Inc.,
3117 North 7th Street, West Monroe, Louisiana 71291-2227

ISBN 1-878990-78-0

Jacket and interior design by LinDee Loveland.
Cover photography by Doug Hopfer
Manuscript editing by Philis Boultinghouse

Scripture quotations not otherwise marked are from the New International Version, © 1973, 1978, 1984 by International Bible Society. Used by permission Zondervan Bible Publishers. Other Scripture references are from the following sources: New American Standard Bible (NASB), © 1973 by The Lockman Foundation; the King James Version (KJV), © 1961 The National Publishing Co.

Tropical Storm © Aris Multimedia Entertainment, Inc. 1991–3.

Dedication

To my children—Israel, Annē, Hannah, Glory, Judah, Galen, Raina, Asa, and Ezra . . . that they may be constantly reminded of their heritage in Christ Jesus

To my wife, Melinda—that she may be reminded that joy is in the journey and that we are in the journey together

To all the hurting and disillusioned people— that they may be reminded that the mighty love of God transcends any wounding, that his cleansing is deep, and that with God nothing is impossible

Contents

✦

CONTENTS

Foreword

It is my firm conviction that as God has advanced his purposes throughout history, it has been his pleasure to accompany his preached Word with prophetic music. This gift of God confirms and validates the preached word and provides a means of expression and continuity in times of God's special moving.

In Dennis Jernigan we find, in my opinion, a special instrument, painfully prepared in the fires of adversity and forged through that heat into a rare instrument of psalmic worship.

Dennis is my friend, and my heart as a father beats with excitement over what God has done and is doing in and with him as he grows more and more into a "worship statesman" among us.

This volume, which reveals the perilous path that made Dennis a worshiper and a steadfast "God-gazer," is a must read for anyone whose heart beats with a passion to know and experience real worship.

I am pleased to recommend a reading of this work to everyone and predict for it a long and productive life.

Jack Taylor

Author and Pastor
Dimensions Ministries

Acknowledgments

I would like to thank:

God Almighty—for the blood of Jesus that washed me clean, the embrace of the Holy Spirit who does not leave me to live this life alone, and for the intimate fellowship I have found in my relationship to my Creator—for the mystery of his majesty.

Howard Publishing—for the heart of ministry and desire to bless people—and for believing in me and making me feel valued.

John Howard—for the opportunity to share my heart so freely to such a wide audience.

Gary Myers—for pursuing me first as a friend and then as a writer.

Philis Boultinghouse—for editing by the leadership of the Holy Spirit. You have shattered all the myths of horror I once believed about editors. Thank you for capturing my heart and making it flow from the pages.

ACKNOWLEDGMENTS

Kathy Law—for everything. I could not do what I do without your help. You are a true friend.

Robert and Peggy (Dad and Mom)—for your willingness to allow me to share my heart so freely, even when it hurts. Thank you for always believing in me and for always being there for me. You are both a part of all God is doing in my life and ministry—whether you like it or not!

Trish Pfeifer—for being the initial instrument God used to get this book started, for "bumping" into Gary Myers! Thank you for helping keep the office together and for loving Jesus.

Robin Jamison—for being such a radiant voice in the office. I am grateful for the heart you display to those who call. You are a conduit of God's majesty.

Jack Taylor—for being a hero and an inspiration to put my heart in writing.

Chuck Angel—for believing in me and for challenging me to deeper places in the mystery of God's majesty. You are a true friend.

New Community Church—for being a fertile garden where I can sow the seeds of my heart. Thank you for being a birthplace for music and for taking care of me and my family. Thank you for letting me practice what I preach on you guys!

Israel, Annē, Hannah, Glory, Judah, Galen, Raina, Asa, and Ezra—for being God's gifts to me and for being vessels of inspiration and reflections of God's majesty in my life.

Melinda—for being the wife I had always dreamed of, whose worth is far above material riches. You are living proof of God's majesty in my life.

Something You Should Know Before You Read On

At an early age, I became involved in sexual immorality (homosexuality), which enveloped my being well into young adulthood. The reasons were many. Suffice it to say, I had a warped understanding of God. My father was not openly affectionate toward me. He was a good provider and always present in my life—I just never heard him verbally express love or approval of me; I only heard the verbal expressions of how I failed him.

As a result, I came to believe it was my performance that would make me acceptable and pleasing to him. My life became one, long obsession to gain his love and approval. The need for fatherly approval became intertwined with my sexual identity and resulted in perversion. I simply believed a lot of lies from a very early age—lies about my father and lies about myself. Looking back, it is very easy to see that many and constant were my father's expressions of love for me, I just did not see them at the time. I have now learned the truth—but more importantly, I have put on that truth.

During this same time in my life, I discovered that God had gifted me musically—so much so that I was the church pianist from the time I was nine years old. I was often called a "sissy" and had all other manner of insults heaped upon me—insults that are often placed upon a little boy who happens to play the piano. In addition to this, I knew that what I struggled with sexually was a sin. I just did not know how to overcome it at the time.

I often heard "church people" talk about what needed to be done with homosexuals—like ship them all out of the country—and I heard them say that all homosexuals belonged in hell. Hearing this from my elders, I felt I had no place to go for help. The church was the last place I felt I could go. The world sounded more loving and accepting. My resultant conclusion was that God was like my perception of my father and the church—unapproachable, harsh, and totally disgusted with who I was.

After college, my life came crashing to the bottom. The Lord met me there with the love and forgiveness I had only dreamed about. He led me into the deepest intimacy I have ever known.

The fact that he allowed me to know him and to be known by him—and the realization that I have not even begun to tap into the full extent of all he is—this is the epitome of majesty to me. He cleansed me of my sin with his redeeming blood and filled my life with overcoming grace—so much grace that I am a married man and the father of nine children—so much redemption that my father now works with me in my ministry to others!

Father God has taken me on an incredible journey of discovery—a discovery of his great depths and, along the way, a discovery of who I am. He continues to redeem my past in ways I never thought possible. There were many times in my life when I perceived that God had abandoned me. But as I have sought to know him, I have come to realize that he can even redeem those old memories of abandonment by revealing to me *his* perspective on those situations and circumstances.

A few years ago, I took a worship team back to minister in the town where I grew up. After the service, an older woman approached me with these words: "Isn't it wonderful how your grandmother's prayers have been answered?" My grandmother had died when I was twelve years old, and I had no memories of any prayers for me.

I told the woman, "I have no idea what you are talking about. But would you please tell me?"

She asked me if I remembered the times—almost daily—when I would go to my grandmother's house and play the piano. I told her that I did, indeed, remember those precious times. She then told me that whenever I would play the piano at her house, my Grandmother Jernigan would stand behind me and pray for me—she prayed that God would use me in the area of worship and music for his glory!

I was overwhelmed with joy and gratitude as I thought about all that God had done in my life. Immediately, the

Holy Spirit reminded me of all the times, even as a twelve-year-old, when I felt that God had forsaken me. But now he gently said, "See. I was there all the time. I loved you so much that I even had others praying for you, and you didn't even know it." What joy! What a loving God. What majesty.

Now that you know a little more about my perspective, perhaps you, like me, will be able to learn to see life and its many ups and downs from a different perspective than the enemy of God presents. It is my prayer that you and I, together, learn to see our lives from Father God's point of view.

> From those heights, the view can be
>> quite enlightening,
>> quite life-changing,
>> quite glorious,
>> quite breathtaking.

All that he is, we cannot contain. Yet he has chosen to live his life in and through us. This is simply one small, yet miraculous, display of the mystery of his great majesty.

Prelude

The *unapproachable* has a magnetic effect upon the human heart.

A thing that is bigger than we are—a thing of majesty or splendor—draws us to know its grandeur in an intimate way. Perhaps we feel that in climbing that mountain or in exploring that ocean, we will somehow come to a deeper understanding of our own identity—find the reason for our very existence.

Majesty begins with a recognition of the enormity, the significance, the splendor of some object or person. The word *majesty* denotes something meriting the highest praise or regard—like a king or president or some other important dignitary. When I think of *majesty,* my mind is immediately flooded with words like greatness, glory, magnificence, stateliness, nobility—and these words are accompanied by pictures of high mountain peaks, vast expanses of ocean, or kings reigning from gilded palaces—all seemingly unapproachable; all alluring.

Majesty takes on a whole new dimension when we actually have the privilege of entering the presence of the admired object or person. To finally see someone we greatly respect or hold in the highest place of honor is indeed an awesome thing. To be in such a presence causes our hearts to beat a little faster and even takes our breath away.

Majesty moves to the deepest level possible when we finally interact with our object of awe. For the one who scales the high mountain, it is like becoming one with its grandeur, and thus empowered to climb even higher places—which become visible only from the mountaintop. For the one who actually sits with the long-admired hero, it is like suddenly living in a dream that had seemed absolutely unreachable only moments before—much like a school girl who has listened faithfully to the music of her favorite singer, identifying with each word and note for years, and then one day finding herself across the room from her hero. And then her heart explodes as he beacons her to join him in the candlelight dinner she has always dreamed about. Sheer joy and ecstasy fill her heart. To have an intimate relationship with majesty is the highest level of joy.

Majesty is the feeling we have when we first see something far greater and more powerful than ourselves . . .

like when we realize the immensity and vastness of our God.

Majesty is the feeling we have when we come face
to face with the object of our deepest
longing . . .

like when we realize God desires a relationship
with us in the here and now.

Majesty is the feeling we have when we become one
with the object of our desire . . .

like when we come to know that God's own
Spirit actually lives inside us

Majesty is what we find when we seek to know God
Almighty . . .

"You in me, a mystery of majesty."

ONE

a mystery
of majesty

A Mystery of Majesty

Tender, like a melody,
Is the way I've come to know
You love to sing your love to me.
Refreshing like a springtime breeze,
Like the wind, blow through me,
Like the way the wind blows through a tree.
You in me, a mystery of majesty.

Like a deep, refreshing pool in a desert,
To not plunge in I would surely be a fool!
Like the stillness after rain in spring
Is the sureness that in knowing you
My heart has been redeemed!
You in me, a mystery of majesty.

Greater than the highest mountain,
Your majesty! Your majesty!
Deeper than the deepest fountain,
Your majesty! Your majesty!
All that is is only here
Because of who you are!
And here I stand in awe
Of something greater still by far!
Greater than the greatest wonder,
You in me, a mystery of majesty!
You in me, a mystery of majesty!

Soothing, like a child's embrace,
Like the joy I feel to know
The old is gone without a trace!

So humbling, this reality,
All the weight of sin that broke
Your heart upon the Cross for me!
You in me, a mystery of majesty!

INSPIRATION

Psalm 93; 1 Corinthians 3:16–23; Jude 24–25
April 30, 1996

> "Who am I in light of who God is?
> I am overwhelmed at how much he really loves me."

Feeling alone, poured out, and wondering if I was needed, those are the words I journaled to myself when this song was born. They sound painfully like the words I had written to myself concerning the receiving of "The Rhythm of Life."

I have come to recognize many of the patterns the enemy uses in his efforts to get me to fall. That recognition does not necessarily make facing the lies any easier. What does amaze me, though, is the way in which my Father always always comes through in my weakest times with showers and showers of grace! The little bit I know of God is truly the tip of the iceberg and only makes me want to go deeper and deeper into that precious relationship I have with him. How can words adequately describe how he makes me feel? They cannot!

I am overcome with emotion each time I meditate on what he has done for me and in me—the Creator, the God of the Universe, living his life through me? My mind can't begin to fully contain the glory of that revelation.

My smallness, his greatness . . . his glory, and my significance to him . . . this truly is a mystery of majesty.

I would sit down at the piano and begin to play, and I would release my heart through my fingers.

The Lord is my strength and my shield;
my heart trusts in him, and I am helped.
My heart leaps for joy
and I will give thanks to him in song.

Psalm 28:7

A Mystery of Majesty

The enemy has only as much power in my life as I give him. With every temptation, God provides a way of escape—and for me, as a young boy, that escape was the piano.

When I was sad,
    I would play and the sadness would lift.
When I felt lonely,
    I was at the piano.
When I was angry,
    I was at the piano.
When I was depressed,
    I was at the piano.

When I was happy or joyful,
 I was at the piano.

I would sit down at the piano and begin to play, and I would release my heart through my fingers. Even on warm summer days, when most were outside, I could be found pounding out my heart at the piano. In the winter, the piano was a warming refuge for me. My grandmother often enticed me to play when it was freezing outside by saying, "Dennis, come in here and warm up your fingers after your chores are done." And that was about all the convincing I needed to practice! In talking with others who began playing an instrument at an early age, I am one of the few I know who were actually disciplined for practicing too much!

I felt peace and fulfillment when I played.
 I felt refuge from the harsh realities of my life.
 I felt God's presence.

But that was practically the only time I felt his presence. Most of the time, I believed that God was a harsh being, concerned only with my performance and interested in me only when I messed up. It never occurred to me that there was something wrong with this picture: feeling God's peace when I played, yet feeling his displeasure the rest of the time. I should have known that the God whose presence I experienced when I played was a God of peace—no matter what I did! It would take years of bondage and suffering to realize who the real ministers of harshness in my life were—namely, the enemy of God and me!

Looking back at the refuge the piano was for me, I think of the way King Saul must have felt when he was tormented by evil spirits and would call for the shepherd boy to play his harp. With every stroke of those strings, David played his heart before the king and the evil was driven away. That must have been what God was doing in my life. I must have been very tormented, because it seems I was always at the piano.

I didn't know it yet, but God had provided the piano as a very unique and fitting escape. As a boy, I assumed my talents were simply an accident of nature, but I understand now that God had placed within my very identity a means of approaching him that involved my entire being. Playing before him involved my mind . . . my emotions . . . my physical body . . . and my deepest being.

I find it no great mystery, now, to see why the enemy would try so desperately to keep me from playing. When the taunts and name calling would come, I would go for periods of time without playing because I didn't want to be known as a sissy or a freak. Yet, something always eventually drew me back to those keys. I guess one might say that God gave me the "keys" to my own heart!

I used to make up little melodies, often dreaming that maybe someday I could write songs that others would find pleasing and enjoyable. I just didn't realize what getting to that point would require.

I didn't realize that God would allow my heart to become so broken.

I didn't know he would allow me to go through such intense pain.

I didn't comprehend that he would allow me to walk in sin or that he would allow the enemy to torment me as he did.

I didn't understand that healing comes through pain.

I didn't fathom the possibility that joy comes through sorrow.

I didn't even entertain the possibility that purity comes through fire . . .

>that quenching comes after dry deserts,

>that sustenance comes after famine,

>that freedom comes after bondage,

>that springtime comes after the harsh, cold winter.

And I didn't understand that all of this was for a *reason.* God used the canvass of my life to paint a picture of redemption; he used the blank pages of my heart to write a heavenly symphony—*the song of the redeemed.*

Like the prodigal son who had run far away from his father, I, too, had run away. And like the prodigal, I had squandered all my inheritance and exchanged it for a lie. I found myself eating the refuse of life with the swine. Once at the bottom, I began to long for home—for the voice of my Father—and then I heard him singing . . . tender, like a melody of grace that said, "Son, come home. I am here, and I've been waiting for you. It doesn't matter where or how far you've fallen.

Let me wash you in my cleansing blood.

Let me clothe you in my robe of righteousness.

Let me feed your hungry soul with my Bread of Life.

Let me bind up your wounds with my joy.

Let me quench your thirst with my Living Water.

Let me warm the coldness of life with the fire of my passion for you.

Let me walk with you in life's journey.

Let me sing over you."

I had not realized how much I needed a Savior until I realized how lost I had been. I had not been able to hear the song of redemption until I had sung the song of the captive. But like a newborn baby whose cries are calmed by the song of a daddy, my heart was brought to peace and calm when my ears finally were opened to the song of the Redeemer.

Like those cold winter days when I would warm my hands at my grandmother's piano, my heart, once bound in the winter of sin and made bitter by the cold, was now warmed by the song of a King.

Instead of being constantly swayed by hard, winter winds, I was now free to be refreshed by a gentle breeze blowing from the heart of Almighty God. My heart, like a tree in a springtime breeze, was free to bud with new life—the bitterness was driven away, the sap of new life began to flow, and the life became visible . . . because now, the wind of the Spirit had something to blow through!

God in me.

A mystery of majesty.

ONE: A MYSTERY OF MAJESTY

MEDITATION

- How does the enemy capture your mind and emotions?
- What ways of escape has God provided you to supersede the will of the enemy?
- When the enemy wants you to focus on the problems or the trials, what does God want you to focus on?
- How does God desire to drive away the lies in your life?
- Has he given you any unique ways to flood your soul with the peace of his presence?

He gives to his beloved

"Even in their sleep . . ."
PSALM 127:2 NASB

Ask the Lord to let you hear him singing over you even while you sleep.

Discovering
the depth of
God's heart
made me want
to plunge
deeper still.

The burning sand will become a pool,
the thirsty ground bubbling springs.

Isaiah 35:7

Plunge In

As far back as my very earliest recollection, my family spent a lot of time on the Illinois River in northeastern Oklahoma. In fact, it was quite sometime before I realized this was not our own private body of water!

I knew every inch of the five-mile stretch where we spent our summers. I could tell you where the swiftest water ran and where the shallow spots were. I could take you to the deep pools where the biggest fish lay hidden and where, in the heat of the summer, the coolest water could be found.

When we were small, we were confined to the boat ramp area—the boring shallow water. But even though the water was shallow, there were still a lot of discoveries to be made. The little minnows were like sharks to us—like wild animals waiting to be stalked and stealthily captured. We delighted ourselves in splashing around in the shallow water and even experienced the sensations of what it felt like to float on our "life rafts"—our inner tubes—in deep water. Our inner tubes were symbols of power. The bigger the tube, the more power we felt we had (even though the big, showy tubes were actually slower and less maneuverable.) Yes, we had fun and many memories were made, but we longed for the day when we could explore the mysteries of the deep waters.

The end of the ramp symbolized the mysterious adventures that awaited us. We were allowed to go to the end and no further. We could feel the edge with our toes and even dangle perilously over the edge—but to go beyond was to endanger our lives (not to mention our behinds). To go farther, we had to mature and we had to learn to swim. But how could we learn to swim if we never went farther? And once we learned to swim, how could we go farther if we were too afraid of what might be out there?

Isn't the spiritual life like that? Many people are content to stay in the shallows, occasionally testing the end of their ramp with their toes but quickly heading back for shore when the deep waters bring fear. They may even have flashy water toys (like impressive degrees or important status), but really, all they are doing is playing in their comfort zones. Shallow waters are fun—for awhile. But let that shallow-water kid get his first glimpse of all the possibilities of the deep waters, and he will discover how boring and lifeless the shallow waters really are.

The first time I saw my cousin dare to swim across the river and then beckon for me to follow, I was mortified. All I could think of was what my parents would say. Even after receiving their permission to try that initial crossing, I was hesitant. Was it really possible to get there? Wouldn't it be better to be satisfied with what I knew? What if a snake tried to get me? What if I didn't have the strength to get there?

But my questions didn't last long. The sounds of joy and triumph from my cousin as he conquered the river peaked my desire to plunge in. And then I did it!

I plunged in! I had never dreamed of all the possibilities! On the other side were forests waiting to be explored. On the other side was refuge from the girls! On the other side was my destiny! After that first plunge, my confidence grew. As my confidence grew, my parents gave me even more freedom. Not only could I now swim across the river, I could go up or down it in either direction as far as I desired!

We never would have discovered the old sunken boat had I not plunged in. I never would have realized the sensation of flying had I not gone beneath the surface of the deep pools. I never would have grown in my abilities had I stayed satisfied with the shallows. Following our dreams—risking our lives— brought so many rewards that we felt foolish for ever wanting to stay in the shallows.

Mind you, there is nothing wrong with shallow water— there is simply only so far you can go when relegated to the edge. With God, it is no different. We can live our lives in the shallow waters of his character and presence—or we can journey to some of the deepest mysteries of his identity. To have the deepest river of God available to our hearts yet never to plunge in would be like choosing to stay in the scorching heat of the desert when a cool, refreshing pool was there for the taking. To have the depths of Almighty God just waiting for our entrance and yet not take advantage of it by plunging in is foolish. The heart that doesn't desire to know more of God is a foolish heart.

On the day God revealed his heart of love for me, he gave me a vision of what the journey of my life was all about —a vision of what my life could be if I would simply plunge into his deep heart. I had known years of dryness and shallowness, but on this day, he gave me a vision of refreshing, deep possiblities.

> I allowed myself to fly upward, and then, like a missile, I plunged downward into the center of God's heart.

In this vision, his heart was represented by a deep, emerald-green pool. His Spirit was represented by a strong, fast horse of purest white. I saw myself riding upon that horse— around and around the inside edges of the pool. I never allowed the horse to take me beyond the shallow edges. It was fun to simply stay up on his back and ride around! Yet something compelled me to begin running deeper. And before I knew it, I was on a high diving board jumping up and down with all my might. When I reached the highest I could possibly jump, I allowed myself to fly upward and then, like a missile, I plunged downward into the center of God's heart.

As I sank, I felt free to let go of all inhibitions—to be totally honest. The deep waters flooded into every recess of my heart and washed out all manner of debris. Along with this cleansing, my grave clothes began to fall away from my body. Everything that hindered my downward freefall was stripped away. Finally, I found myself naked in his presence—yet unashamed. Not only had I been cleansed, but I had been refreshed and invigorated as well.

Discovering the depth of God's heart made me want to plunge deeper still. I no longer desired the shallow places. I only desired to know him more; I would never again be content to splash around in the shallows of life. To stay in the shallowness would be foolish in light of the vast, unexplored regions of all God is—in light of understanding more about who I was created to be and all God desired for me to be. If I shied away from the depths—if I chose not to plunge in—my life might be sustained . . . but would that really be *living?*

M E D I T A T I O N

- Are you in the shallows, or are you in the depths of God?

- How can you get to the deeper places of God?

- How can you get to the deeper places of your own identity?

- What are some of your fears concerning going deeper with God?

- What are your fears concerning discovering the deeper places of your own heart?

"Even in their sleep . . ."
Psalm 127:2 NASB

Ask the Holy Spirit to reveal any fears you have concerning your walk with him. Ask him to show you how to let go and plunge in!

Some of the most

impacting memories are

of the small moments

with which God sprinkles

our lives.

God has chosen to make known . . .
the glorious riches of this mystery,
which is Christ in you,
the hope of glory.
Colossians 1:27

Simplicity of Majesty

When I think of majesty, my mind naturally gravitates toward the gigantic and grand—

the Grand Canyon at sunset,

the ocean at dawn,

a tall mountain on a clear day,

a thunderstorm on the distant horizon.

But God's majesty—his massiveness—cannot be relegated to, or contained in, something so large. He is so incredible in his creativity that his majesty can be displayed in some of the smallest wonders in the universe.

Take, for instance, the ingredients God has ordained for the conception of life. Man contributes only one small cell; woman contributes another; yet when these two microscopic cells join and their genetic codes are released, a new being comes miraculously into existence. Everything that will one day be recognizable as a human being is already in that newly formed minuscule creation—all ordained and put into motion by the majesty of God. Majesty comes in small packages too.

God's majesty is displayed in dynamic and unexpected ways. Take, for instance, the tiny ant. Able to lift a load equal to many times its own body weight, this tiny dynamo, when compared to our human abilities, is mightier than the strongest human known. Working in union within a complex societal order, the ant builds super ant-highways, stores enough food to sustain a colony of thousands through the winter, cares for the sick and injured, and watches out for the overall welfare of the colony. And all of this is done in an orderly fashion, with the utmost resourcefulness, nothing going to waste, and all without ever saying an audible ant-word! Try to accomplish something so monumental on a human scale! Majesty comes in small packages.

The majesty of God is overwhelmingly demonstrated in the state of being we call *life*. We normally think of humans when we think of life, but have you ever contemplated the wonders that are contained in a single drop of water taken from a pond? Within that one tiny drop, a multitude of God's handiworks exists. Not only can every manner of germ and microbe be found in this single drop, but also tiny one-celled creatures that live and breath and procreate and give sustenance to the larger creatures like crawfish or minnows. These creatures, in turn, give sustenance to even larger creatures (that food chain thing, you know!).

It staggers my mind to think that my existence and sustenance could depend upon something I can't even see with my naked eye (my clothed eye is no better!). If each form of life did not receive life from another, no species would survive. Even the smallest plants are fed by the waste from the smallest animal. Our own digestive system would not function properly without the intestinal flora and fauna found in each human being's digestive tract! Life depends upon life. Life comes in small packages, and life—no matter how insignificant—is an expression of God's might and majesty.

Some of my favorite memories have come from witnessing magnificent performances—whether the performance is by a person using a God-given talent or by a majestic streak of lightning that shatters the darkness of the blackest night. Yet, some of the most impacting memories are of the small moments with which God sprinkles our lives.

As that performer leaves the stage and I am left to contemplate with awe the effect of one small word or one exquisite turn of a melody or phrase, it is not the performance I necessarily remember, but how the performance affected me. Joy and peace come from knowing that we have been touched by God through some small thought or satisfaction.

After the sounds of the powerful storm subside—the loud rushing of the wind, the pounding of the rain, and the explosions of thunder—after these have passed us by, we are confronted with another sound—the sound of silence. Silence seems insignificant in comparison to a mighty storm, but it is in the silence that we are flooded with the sounds of our hearts reminding us that the Maker of Storms is also the Bringer of Peace. Which is more powerful, the storm or the peace that follows? Small often equals mighty. Thoughts of majesty come in small packages, left by big moments on the doorsteps of our hearts.

What about one single thought? Have you ever thought of a thought as being a tangible part of God's majesty? With one thought, we can be overwhelmed. What about the thoughts of a mother when one of her little ones is hurt or hungry? Consumed with one thought and one thought alone—to see the needs of her child met—that mother will forgo her own welfare to see that child fed or ministered to. One thought.

With one single thought, a life can be taken. Why does a person take his own life? While there are many reasons why a man may choose to take his life, doesn't it really boil down to one thought—one silent, mental choice—to give up, to bring an end to some deep, unsubsiding pain?

With one thought, a life can be held captive by the enemy of God. Have you ever believed something terrible about yourself? Have you ever had a deceitful thought shattered by the truth of God? With one thought, a mind can be set free.

With one thought, the mind of God imagined a whole universe and still held you and I in highest regard while speaking it all into existence. Majesty comes in incredibly simple ideas.

Mighty displays of nature are insignificant when compared to the wonder a mother feels the first time she holds her first baby . . . or the dumbstruck feeling a father feels the first time his little boy reaches for his embrace.

One sin separated me from my God.

One crucifixion among thousands transformed the lives of fallen men and woman.

One drop of blood cleansed me and paid my debt.
One sinner, among millions, saved and transformed
by grace.

God looked from his greatness into the smallness of my
existence and displayed his majesty in redeeming love. The
singular event that changed the world may seem far away and
small—eclipsed by two thousand years of time—yet this distant event reaches into the here and now with every bit of the
resurrection power that was displayed on that first Easter. The
unimaginable massiveness of God now lives in me—small in
the grand scheme of the universe, yet grandly significant in
the mind of the one who made it all!

Show me the highest mountain . . .
its impressiveness pales in the light of redeeming love.
Show me the deepest part of the greatest ocean . . .
it is shallow in comparison to the deep, deep
love and forgiveness found in the gift of
salvation as expressed through Jesus Christ.

All the wonders of the universe combined seem only a vapor
when compared to the breath of God that breathes life into me.
And then that very God displayed his majesty in something
greater still—the human heart that will receive him!

He lives in me! The greatest wonders are often overlooked
because we look for majesty in the "big" things. Majesty is
simple. Look for God in his "small" packages. You may be
surprised by the greatness of their capacity for God!

MEDITATION

- What are some small things you have overlooked that have God's signature all over them?
- How does this view of God's majesty change the value of things in your life?
- How does it change your view of your own identity?
- What impacting memories has God sprinkled in your life?

"Even in their sleep . . ."

Psalm 127:2 NASB

Ask the Lord to take your thoughts to some of the small wonders of life that you may have overlooked.

TWO

I glory in the wonder and the majesty

I Glory in the Wonder
and the Majesty

You move across the strings of my heart
Like the darkest evening sky pierced by a shooting star.
You move across the strings of my heart
Like when meeting face to face a king
    you've known just from afar.
Your majesty is awesome
and piercing to my heart.
I glory in the wonder and
The majesty of who you are.

Your majesty and glory I proclaim—
The wonder and the pow'r
In Jesus name.
In glory and in wonder I proclaim
The majesty and glory of your name.
Your majesty is awesome,
In wonder I proclaim.
I glory in the wonder and
The majesty of Jesus' name!

To feel your presence takes my breath away,
Like to hold your child the first time and
    not quite know what to say.
To feel your presence takes my breath away,
Like a man blind from his birth who fin'lly sees his father's face.
Your majesty is awesome and

Full of love and grace.
I glory in the wonder and
The majesty of your embrace!

INSPIRATION

Psalm 93:1; Hebrews 2:7
July 24, 1991

This song came as I meditated upon some of the most wondrous things I could think of in this life: a dark evening sky made bright by one small shooting star; meeting someone you have looked up to and longed to meet for a very long time; a blind man, once healed, seeing the faces of those he has previously only heard; and holding my sons and daughters for the very first time.

I always meditate on the lives of my children around their birthdays. My oldest son, Israel, celebrates his birthday on July 22. This song was born as I thought about how precious it was to hold my very first child for the very first time. What an awesome and overwhelming feeling that is.

All of these things fill my heart with wonder and really do take my breath away. Yet each one pales in comparison to knowing God. Knowing that my God desires an intimate relationship with me leaves me feeling inadequate to describe how this knowledge makes me feel. Almighty God alive in me—what glory, what majesty, what blessing!

To know you are loved simply
because of who you are and to walk
in that knowledge is a holy thing.

He will rescue them from oppression and violence,
for precious is their blood in his sight.
Psalm 72:14

᠁

Embraced by God

To know you are loved simply because of who you are
and to walk in that knowledge
Is a holy thing.

As a young child, I did not know that kind of love. I never
fully rested in a belief that even my parents loved me.

When I was young, I was often assailed by the enemy. He
is a liar who is opposed to all that God is and all that God
desires to do in us. I was constantly berated by his insults
against my gullible mind. Feelings of inadequacy and a

warped sense of identity got me into sinful bondages at a very early age. This caused great turmoil within my heart because I felt so worthless on the inside. Playing the piano at church on Sunday, then falling into immorality on Monday tore my concept of worth to shreds. As a result, I tried to compensate by performing. If people could just see how much I do and how good I am, perhaps they would love me. Perhaps they would accept me. I would have even settled for believing they liked or tolerated me! I would have settled for someone to just hold me.

I never remember feeling loved by God as a child, and yet I longed to know him and be loved by him. My concept of relationship with him consisted of me trying to please him and of him being distant—at best. My life was a constant parade, marching endlessly to the tune of the lies of the enemy. Outwardly, my life was precise and articulate; inwardly, a storm of tremendous pressure beat my heart against the waves of self-pity and hopelessness; I was headed straight for the reef of death and destruction.

I could not help myself.

After years of being battered, this little boy finally gave up. I found myself stranded on the reef. I could see the shore, and I heard people say there was a God who was a safe harbor. I just couldn't get to him. I no longer had the strength to strive. So I gave up.

Soon, I found myself in the deepest bondage and sin I had ever known. I felt some relief, though, because at least I wasn't being swatted back and forth between the waves. Now I simply gave up to those waves—those sinful impulses—and let them take me wherever they would. I resigned myself to the fact that this was probably all I deserved and all I would know in this life. At least the parade—my charade—could stop. I was a prisoner in the concentration camp of the enemy of God.

But one day, I heard that the camp of the enemy had been conquered by a mighty King and that the King was coming to review all the camp's inhabitants. He was coming to plunder and take the spoils. When I first saw this King, I knew he was a good King. I knew that anyone he chose would find a life of fulfillment and a place of honor. Somehow, I just knew.

But I also knew that I did not deserve any more than I had. My lot was to be just another piece of worthless garbage— refuse—tossed aside and left behind by the King. As he walked down aisle after aisle of the encampment, I saw him pointing to certain people. With each wave of his nail-scarred hand, another prisoner was set free to join the King's entourage. The moments grew into an eternity, and with each beat of my heart, hope rose a little higher. He was close now . . . but would he choose me?

Suddenly, the enemy slipped up behind me and began to whisper, "Don't plan on leaving. He's only taking the things of worth. You're worthless garbage to him, so you might as well forget it!" And my heart began to sob.

Somehow I knew this was my last chance, and now it appeared that my chance was slipping away. The King, indeed, was moving down the lane and toward the harbor. Once there, he would sail to the next encampment and plunder its contents. Dread and fear replaced what little hope I had found, and even these feelings succumbed to a numbing cold as my heart was overwhelmed with sorrow.

But then, out of nowhere, I felt a touch on the shoulder of my heart. Turning to see who would possibly defile himself by touching me, my breath was taken away. I felt as if I had died and gone to heaven. The one whose hand touched me was none other than that of the King. He turned to the enemy and said, "I choose this one as my very own. He belongs to me. He is my prized possession. I have loved him with an everlasting love and have searched far and wide for him. His filth made him unrecognizable, but now he has been cleansed. I want him for my own."

And then the King took me in his arms and held me up for his legions to see. "This is my beloved son, whom I am so pleased to know!"

> Forgiven of my sin.
> Redeemed by the blood of the King.
> Embraced by God.

Only those who understand their redemption can understand how much we have been forgiven and then love accordingly. He who has been forgiven much loves much. Even now, the enemy tries to drag me back to those ways of thinking. His only problem is that now my feet are firmly planted on the rock of another kingdom . . . where I will be forever enveloped in his holy embrace of love.

M E D I T A T I O N

- How much have you been forgiven?
- Did you find God, or did he find you? How does this make you feel?

- What does it mean to you to be embraced by God?
- What are the lies the enemy assails you with?
- How do you overcome his lies? How do you put on truth?

"Even in their sleep . . ."
Psalm 127:2 NASB

Ask the Spirit to remind you of how much you have been forgiven. Then ask him to help you love God to that depth. Ask him to help you see God's embrace upon your own life.

Like a dark, evening sky pierced by a shooting star, God's presence and love took away my spiritual breath.

The Lord is close to the brokenhearted
and saves those who are crushed in spirit.

Psalm 34:18

Shooting Stars

Have you ever stood outside on a clear night and gazed at the stars? Because we live in the middle of nowhere, we have a near-nightly display of God's handiwork without the distraction of city lights. Sometimes I lay down on the ground and search the sky, waiting for a short glimpse of a shooting star. I remember doing this even as a small child, and somehow, the wonder I felt then has followed me into adulthood. I still get just as excited with every streaking trail of fire that pierces the dark evening sky.

I find it difficult to believe there are those who do not acknowledge the existence of God. I cannot look into the reaches of outer space for very long without feeling overwhelmed with a very real awareness and sense of God's *presence*.

Knowing that all I see before me was spoken into existence by one word leaves me awestruck. Knowing that the one who created it all must contain power beyond human comprehension, and knowing, at the same time, that the Creator dwells in my heart is almost too much to fathom.

Growing up, I went through many years of living in what I call "performance mode." As a young boy, I longed for intimacy with God, but the only times I really felt his presence were when I felt guilty—when the conviction of sin would sweep over me without another human being even uttering a word. This told my little boy heart that God only wants to be with me when I mess up . . . because the only time I sensed him was when I messed up. I felt compelled to perform for his acceptance. My performance must mean something, I reasoned, because my bad performance is the only thing that brings me to a place of sensing his presence. I felt a deep desire to please God and to know him intimately; I wanted to be able to be honest with him and not feel overcome with condemnation each time I felt him near . . . but I didn't know how.

As my high school graduation came and college loomed on the horizon, God saw to it that I went to a certain Christian youth camp during the summer between high school and college. I was overwhelmed by the sheer number of young people and marveled at the beauty of the music as it wafted its way through the rafters of the open-air tabernacle and made its way to the heavens. As the guest vocalist began to sing her heart to the Lord, I remember thinking that I had never heard anything so beautiful come from another person's voice as the melodies that floated from the artist that night.

My heart leapt at the thought that, perhaps, I could meet her. Perhaps she would speak to me.

I had heard of Cynthia Clawson but had never heard her sing until that night . . . and I was mesmerized. Her countenance and heart were captivating. Her love for the Lord was obvious. And, in my mind, her celebrity status made her utterly unapproachable by a little nobody like me. Still, I decided I would ask her to sign my Bible. But where to find her? I assumed that a person of her status would be ushered away from the common people and into some fancy reception in her honor behind closed doors. How shocked I was to see her standing directly in my path—talking with other young people!

I cautiously approached her and asked her to sign my Bible, and then I sheepishly stole away, vowing never to erase or otherwise tamper with the precious signature of Cynthia Clawson in my little red King James Bible!

As my college graduation became reality and I found myself empty and directionless, God, once again, intervened with power and grace. During a Second Chapter of Acts concert, God supernaturally overpowered my sin and called me to himself.

Before, I had only known condemnation . . .

Now, I was suddenly bathed in total acceptance.

Before, I felt compelled to hide my heart . . .

Now, I felt suddenly free to be honest.

For the first time . . .

I felt free of the bondages of sin.

For the first time ever . . .

I felt a closeness to God that I had only dreamed about.

God—in my mind—went from being a distant cosmic policeman, waiting to bop me on the head each time I messed up, to a loving, long-suffering, compassionate Father who desired to wash away my filthy sin and bind up my broken heart.

Like a dark, evening sky pierced by a shooting star, God's presence and love took away my spiritual breath. I no longer felt like disappearing into the night whenever he was around. Now I desired to be honest with him . . . because it felt so good!

Like that star-struck high school graduate who was so overcome with emotion at meeting Cynthia Clawson that he couldn't even speak, I was now enjoying an intimate, personal, healing relationship with the God of the universe. This new relationship transcended all my past, overcame all my fears and replaced them with a brand new life, and bathed my heart in healing, cleansing, overwhelming love.

What majesty! What glory it brings my heart to know him!

MEDITATION

- What does God's presence mean to you?
- How would you describe your first realization that God loves you?
- Do you feel you can trust God? Why or why not?
- What things do you need to be honest with God about?

"Even in their sleep . . ."
Psalm 127:2 NASB

Ask the Holy Spirit to "take your breath away" with some aspect of God's presence you have never seen or felt before.

45

This brand-new human being—part me,
part Melinda—was fully capable of
loving and of being loved.
He took my breath away.

O Lord, you have searched me and you know me. . . .
You perceive my thoughts from afar. . . .
You are familiar with all my ways.
Psalm 139:1–3

Breathless

To know and be known by someone greater than
    ourselves
        is the deepest cry of the human heart.
    To know God and to be known by him
        are the goals of every believer.

At certain times in my life, I've felt an intense awareness that
I was known, acknowledged, and blessed by the one greater
than I. I will never forget those epiphanous moments because
they've had a profound effect on my heart and produced eternal change in the depths of my being. Often I didn't recognize
God's hand at the time, but through the years I've seen that
God's ways of dealing with his children are always steeped in
love.

My dad would often take us boys with him to feed the
cows. We loved to ride the tractor on top of the hay or in the

back of the pickup. One day, when I was about four or five, Daddy said he was going to take us with him to the pasture, and I was very excited about going. For some reason, I didn't hear him or my brothers leave the house, but when I heard the pickup truck start, I immediately began to run after it.

I thought I could catch up with them because I knew they had to stop and open the gate, but by the time my little legs got me to the gate, they were already taking off. I kept running after them, crying out, "Wait for me! Wait for me!" But they didn't stop. My five-year-old mind couldn't understand how they could have forgotten me. "Why would my Daddy leave me like that?" I felt so abandoned and rejected, and I allowed the enemy to speak lies into my mind: "They don't really love you"; "They would rather not have you along"; "You're not good enough to go with them anyway." Even though such thoughts bombarded me, I was overjoyed when my dad and brothers came back from their chores. To see them coming in from the pasture and to see my dad's face brought reassurance to my little heart—at least I wasn't alone anymore. Just as seeing them leave me behind had taken my breath away, seeing them return had the same effect!

God wrote that moment on my heart, and I have never forgotten it. Through it, he taught me that just as my earthly father didn't really abandon me, I can be assured that my heavenly Father will never leave me or forsake me. Such moments of realization of God's presence in my life really do take my breath away.

I remember the first time I saw my future wife. That moment will always be frozen in time in the treasure hold of my mind. I had never seen such a beautiful woman. From the moment she walked into the classroom and sat down on the front row, my thoughts were never far from her or my back-row view!

How she took my breath away!

I remember the day I saw her walking arm in arm with her father down the church aisle, looking as if she had been transported from an elegant bridal magazine layout and painted into the picture of my life. Even seeing her veil snagged by one of the pews could not dampen my image of her that day!

She took my breath away.

I remember the day, just three months after our wedding, when Melinda spoke the words, "I think I'm pregnant." One of the dreams of my life becoming a reality was almost too much for my feeble mind to comprehend. A child of my own! How God must love me.

He took my breath away.

I remember seeing the nurse lay my son in the nursery bassinet as she lovingly prepared him for presentation to the world. This brand-new human being—part me, part Melinda —was fully capable of loving and of being loved.

He took my breath away.

And I'll never forget the night God finally set me free from my past and from my sin. For years I had struggled to free myself, but my attempts were in vain. It was as if he were waiting for me to settle down and give up my striving. It appears to me that when I finally gave up, he sovereignly stepped in and called me to his side. All I had to do was accept his proposal.

I will never forget seeing him
>   accept my sin (homosexuality) and place it on
>   the shoulders of Jesus Christ.

I will never forget seeing him
>   suffer my death and humiliation on the Cross.

I will never forget how he
>   died, paid my debt, and was buried with my
>   sin and failure.

I will never forget how I
>   was crucified and buried with him.

I will never forget the moment I
>   heard him calling me to rise up from my old
>   life.

I will never forget him telling me
>   to leave the old Dennis in the grave
>   and come forth and walk as the new creation
>   he had made me to be!

I will never forget how he
>   began teaching me who he is
>   and who I really am.

To know and delight in him is awesome. But to be known by him and to realize that he takes more delight in me than I could possibly take in him is incomprehensible. It takes my breath away! It was as if I had been blind my whole life and then had my sight miraculously restored. The moment I saw my Father's face of mercy and forgiveness—the moment I realized he would love me no matter what—my life was radically and irrevocably changed forever!

Knowing God takes my breath away!

MEDITATION

- What takes your breath away?
- Do you ever have feelings of "breathlessness" with God? Why or why not?
- What are some of the epiphanies of your life?
- Why are these moments so memorable to you?
- What areas of your life would you like to see God touch in a profound and memorable way?

"Even in their sleep . . ."

Psalm 127:2 NASB

Ask the Lord to take your breath away—to breathe new life into the stale places of your life. Rest in his presence.

Rohi
Jehova
Shalom
Nissi
M'Kadd

Knowing what
our Father is
like gives us
clues as to how
we are supposed to be.

O Lord, our Lord, how majestic is your name
in all the earth!

Psalm 8:9

The Glory of
Who You Are

I revel in the raw immensity of all God is,
because I recognize that all he is lives in me!

To *glory* in the wonder of who God is, is to rejoice triumphantly in the victory God has won for us over sin through Jesus Christ. I rejoice and exult in my God, the one who has far exceeded my hopes and my dreams—and I want to *know* him more intimately.

One of the first ways we get to know someone is by learning his or her name. Soon that name becomes so identified with that person that we associate the character qualities of the individual with his or her name. Subsequently, every time we hear a certain name we think, "John—he's a servant," or "Chuck—what a fun guy," or "Kathy is so thoughtful." You get the picture. Yet, how sad that we, as believers, often go our whole lives without taking the time to learn the many names of our God—for it is by his *names* that we know his *character.*

When we know what God is like, we are able to trust him more. Furthermore, knowing what our Father is like gives us clues as to how we are supposed to be. God's Word tells us that his name is a strong tower where the righteous can run and be safe (Prov. 18:10). His Word also tells us that a good name is to be more desired than great riches (Prov. 22:1). Our God is much more awesome than we ever imagined. The number of names we could use to describe him are as endless as he is. For brevity's sake, we'll look at just a few of the ways he reveals his character to us through some of the names he calls himself in Scripture.

He Is *Jehovah* (Exodus 3:14)

I Am . . .

Who I Am

Self-existent

This is the God who was and is and always will be—and amazingly, he lives in us! Jesus said that he and the Father are one and that he would send us the Holy Spirit—this is part of our heritage. We are the children of this eternal God. We are created in his image, redeemed by the blood of Jesus

Christ, and filled with the power of the Holy Spirit to be conduits of God's love and blessing to others. The name *Jehovah,* when coupled with other descriptive names of God, reveals his true nature. We'll look at just a few.

He is *Jehovah-tsidkenu* (Jeremiah 23:5–8)
I Am . . .

> Righteous
> Life
> Redemption

This is the God who reveals himself to us in righteousness, who is our life-giver, the one who redeems. Jesus was revealed to be our righteousness: "God made him [Jesus] who had no sin to be sin for us, so that in him we might become the righteousness of God" (2 Cor. 5:21). Jesus came as the Way, the Truth, and the Life. He came as Redeemer, making a way for us to be restored to God.

He is *Jehovah-rohi* (Psalm 23)
I Am . . .

> Shepherd
> Guide
> Protector
> Exhorter

We were all like sheep, gone astray (Isa. 53). God painted this picture beautifully for us through Jesus as he gave himself for us as the sacrificial Lamb who washed away the sins of the world (John 10:11).

He is *Jehovah-rophe* (Exodus 15:26)

I Am . . .

> Healer
>
> Health
>
> Healing
>
> Physician

Many times throughout Old Testament Scripture, Father came as Healer. Nothing changed with the advent of Jesus. Nothing has changed today. Healer is who he is (Acts 3:6)!

He is *Jehovah-nissi* (Exodus 17:15)

I Am . . .

> Banner
>
> Victory
>
> Flag
>
> Covering

Just as Aaron and Hur lifted the hands of Moses as a banner over the battle with God's enemies, just as God instructed Moses to lift the brass serpent in the wilderness as a sign of healing and a foreshadowing of the crucifixion, so, too, Jesus was lifted up as our banner of victory on the Cross when he paid the debt we owed for our sins.

He is *Jehovah-jireh* (Genesis 22:14)

I Am . . .

> Provider
>
> Provision

Source
Sufficiency

How can we forget the countless times God provided for his children in the wilderness? How can we not be awestruck by the provision Elijah received from the Lord through the ministry of the ravens and through the widow's remaining dregs of water and flour (1 Kings 17)? Did Jesus not reveal himself to be Provider to that multitude on the hillside there by the Sea of Galilee (John 6:1–14)? He is all we need!

He is *Jehovah-shalom* (Judges 6:24)
I Am . . .
Peace
Comfort
Security

Who can truly know security and peace apart from the Lord? Can human invention and wealth protect us from the ravages of this life? Can the hands and powerful medicines of the earthly physician give us hope and security for the whole of eternity? Who is the one who calmed the raging sea? Was it not Jesus? We have the hope of his peace now if we will accept him for who he truly is (Phil. 4:6–7).

He is *Jehovah-shammah* (Ezekiel 48:35)
I Am . . .
Omnipresent
God Is There
Friend

Faithfulness

Strength

As the psalmist so eloquently reminds us in Psalm 139, there is nowhere we go where he is not. Where can we go that he cannot reach? Just as the Father is always there, Jesus in us is our hope of glory. He will not leave us, and he will never forsake us—no matter what (Col. 1:27; Heb. 13:5, 8).

*H*e is *Jehovah M'Kaddesh* (Leviticus 20:7)

I Am . . .

Holiness

Sanctity

Light

As believers, we have each been set apart and sanctified for his purposes in and through us. We belong to him (1 Pet. 2:9–10). We often get ourselves into trouble as sheep when we compare ourselves to other sheep. Indeed, one sheep may appear to be whiter on the surface than the next, but let the pure white snow fall on the field and the real color of each sheep is dingy and dirty compared to the bright, pure white of the snow. God alone is holy and pure and without sin. Jesus alone, through his shed blood, makes us holy. His light reveals not only our way in the darkness but our deep need for him and his power (1 John 1:7).

How can we glory and rejoice in someone we barely know? How much greater will our rejoicing, wonder, and glory be when we understand more and more of who our God is and what he is like. How much more will we be able to overcome trials when we discover—because of who he is and whose we are—

who we are because of him.

M E D I T A T I O N

- In what ways does God's name affect how you feel toward him?
- How does this make you feel toward Jesus?
- What does your name mean?
- What would you like others to think about when they hear your name?
- How was the character of God (his names) revealed in the life of Christ Jesus?

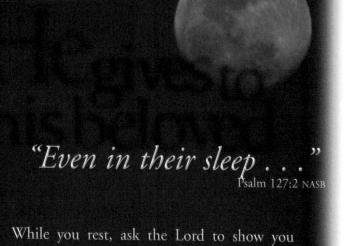

"Even in their sleep . . ."

Psalm 127:2 NASB

While you rest, ask the Lord to show you some aspect of his nature you have never seen before.

THREE

I like it that way

I Like It That Way

Just when I think I know you,
You go and surprise me
With a part of you I've not seen.
Like ev'ry day's a birthday
Party here inside me
You are simply more than I dreamed.

You are more than I had ever hoped for,
More than I had ever dreamed of,
More than any joy my words might convey.
You are more with ev'ry day I know you,
More than I could ever show you,
More than anything, you're worthy of praise.
I like it that way!

Even through the hard times,
Darkness all around me,
You come shining showing the way.
The more I get to know you,
You grow more astounding,
Surprising with your presence each day.

You are like the dawn ev'ry morning,
Chasing all the darkness away.
Like a present, you're unwrapping before me,
Revealing a little more day by day—day by day!

INSPIRATION

Psalm 98; 1 Corinthians 2:9
December 13, 1995

One of my best friends in the world, Matt Vandiver, is also my worship leader at New Community Church. During one of our conversations about all God is doing in us and in New Community Church, Matt confessed he struggles at times with feeling needed. I felt impressed to simply begin listing all the ways I could see how vital his life is to the body of Christ, and we basically began to exhort one another and build each other up. After we had talked for over an hour, we hung up the phone and God began to give me the stirrings of this song. "I Like It That Way" came as I focused on God's plan for Matt's life—from my perspective. God has gifted Matt deeply, yet the enemy tries to mislead him. God showed me that he wanted to take even Matt's hard times and surprise Matt with his presence. Matt has a lot of little sayings, and the phrase "I like it that way" is something he would say. This song came as I prayed for Matt and sang over his situation. It is a song of rejoicing in the fact that no matter how difficult life gets, God is more than we ever dreamed. Sort of makes you want to seek him that much more, doesn't it?

Jesus living his life in and through me makes every day a surprise party.

Come and see what God has done,
how awesome his works in man's behalf!
Psalm 66:5

More Than
I Hoped For

When I was a little boy, I looked forward to each birthday with great anticipation and cautious hope. I dreamed of a *surprise* birthday party. But every year, the day would come and go, and there would be no surprise party. Oh, I would get presents and a cake, and sometimes even a party, but there was no surprise.

I finally gave up my dream.

When I went off to college and found that most of my new friends felt just as far away from home as I did, I often took great pleasure in helping to plan and pull off surprise parties for others. But there was no such party for me.

Imagine my shock and surprise when I walked into a darkened dorm lobby—on yet another lonely, surpriseless birthday—only to have the life scared out of me with that thunderous, wonderful shout of "Surprise!" To me, their raucous noise sounded like a heavenly choir. With every smile and gift presentation, I was reduced to tears. No words could adequately express the joy in my heart. My senses experienced a wonderful overload.

Suddenly I realized that all I had known and experienced of birthdays up until that moment was but a glimpse of reality. At that instant, I was taken by the heart and ushered into a new realm of experience.

My early experiences with knowing God were much like the feelings of that little boy who had no idea what a surprise birthday party was like. I had a knowledge of God and had even felt his presence in many church services, but he never *surprised* me. And deep down, I believed that he didn't really love or accept me and that he really was not very interested in my life. I wanted a God who would respond to me as *I* desired and who would give me what I wanted—and I was disappointed when he didn't. My expectations were born to be crushed! As a result, I grew to believe that I had experienced all of God there was and that I knew him as well as I could in this life.

But as I grew to manhood, life and its sorrows taught me that I needed much more from God than having my childhood desires fulfilled. I required a much bigger God than I had ever known. But the God I knew was not big enough to help me. The God I knew was puny and inadequate. If that was all there was to God, I was lost and without hope. Like an inexperienced sailor, I believed that the iceberg above the water was all there was.

Where can you turn when you are overcome with feelings of rejection and failure?

Where will you find shelter when the temptations of life threaten to crush you with the sheer immensity of their weight?

Who do you call when the sins and failures of a lifetime finally drag you to the depths of self-pity and despair?

Just when I thought I had God figured out, I was overwhelmed with years of sin and failure, and my intense need for someone bigger than I had known—or even believed existed—forced me to cry out for help.

And guess what. He surprised me! He taught me that his magnitude—like the iceberg whose immensity lies just below the surface of the water—far exceeded what I had experienced on the surface of life and that he was more than willing to surprise me with his presence!

Jesus living his life in and through me makes every day a surprise party. Every time I try to limit him or reduce him to what I can comprehend, he surprises me with more of him. All that I know of God—all I expect of him—expands with every encounter. He is more than I had ever hoped for . . . more than I had ever dreamed of . . . more than any joy my words might convey. Whatever I know of God, I can confidently say that he is more!

When overpowered with burdens and failures that push you under the raging waters again and again . . .

you need someone with a long reach and strong arm.

When destructive feelings threaten to destroy your identity . . .

you need someone who has the power to change your identity.

You need one thing, pure and simple. . .

you need Jesus Christ.

You need to be surprised by God.

MEDITATION

- What burdens overpower you and threaten to pull you under?

- In what ways have you limited God in your life?

- When was the last time you were surprised by some aspect of God that you had not seen or experienced before?

He gives to his beloved

"Even in their sleep . . ."

Psalm 127:2 NASB

As you prepare for bed, ask the Holy Spirit to
meet with you there and to surprise you with his
presence. Ask him to help you see him as you wake;
ask him to surprise you with a deeper awareness of
his presence in your life.

How often we miss his
little surprises because
we only see from our
limited perspective—we
don't see the view from
God's heart.

What is man that you are mindful of him,
the son of man that you care for him?

Psalm 8:4

⁂

Surprise! Surprise! Surprise!

Knowing God is an adventurous journey. One moment we are enjoying a grand and scenic view of some aspect of God never seen before and the very next we are clinging for dear life to a thin rope, while dangling over a sheer cliff with a five-thousand-foot vertical drop! This is life. The journey of life, simply put, is getting to know God through every experience and from various vantage points.

Knowing God is made possible only by virtue of the blood of Jesus. When we were separated from God by our sin, Jesus took our sin upon himself and was crucified. He was buried and raised again by resurrection power, and it is that very same power that changes our identities and makes a way for us to know God in an intimate way. Yet, saying we "know" God is like saying we've finally climbed that high mountain we've always admired from afar. Yet when we get to the pinnacle, we realize that this "high mountain" was just one small hill in the vast range of who God is!

Considering our feeble attempts at relationship with God, it is incredibly awesome that God—the Creator of the universe—desires fellowship with me—one little drop in the ocean of all he has created. He desires to live his life in me and through me! What majesty!

Whether we are experiencing moments of ecstatic joy or seasons of dark despair, our majestic and mighty God constantly pours out his grace and power to meet our changing needs with his unchanging love. What a journey! What a majestic God!

During the darkest period of my life, I came to the day when I gave up on God. I saw no power or change in my own life, even though I had begged him to change me. But the fault was mine—not his. Because of my limited perspective of who he is and because I had become so focused on me and my needs, I was blinded to the view of me from God's heart. But all that changed the night someone found out my sin and confronted me.

The one thing I had hoped to keep hidden—that thing I knew would ruin my reputation and devastate my life—was brought into the light of truth . . . and I was scared. Now I would be utterly and forever rejected—not only by God, but by those who knew me, as well. I ran into the night. I ran until I could run no farther. When I finally stopped, I wept. All I could think of was that I had nowhere to run and nowhere to hide. Every security and every mask I had worn was now torn from my heart, and I was left exposed—naked and ashamed.

I was at the end of myself. My heart was broken, and I desperately needed someone bigger than me to step in and heal my heart. I simply asked God for his help.

As I gazed into the starry expanse of the heavens, my eyes were drawn to a solitary cloud. Something inside me told me to look beyond the physical and into the spiritual picture God was trying to paint before me. The cloud appeared to me like the face of an old man with a loving countenance—he had warm, inviting eyes that pierced me deeply and a long, white beard. I then saw a second cloud nearby. This cloud looked like a fluffy, little lamb, and the little lamb

Just when I think I have him figured out, he presents me with yet another gift.

appeared to be wounded and far away from home. In a matter of minutes, the old man cloud engulfed the lamb cloud. I stood there stunned, as I contemplated what I had just seen. I was flooded with the sweet assurance that God wanted to engulf me in the fullness of his love, just as the old man cloud had engulfed the little lamb cloud—totally and unashamedly!

Surprised by his presence. Engulfed in his majesty. I was touched by a God who was big enough to take me to himself and save me. His presence covered my nakedness, and he loved me in spite of my shame.

Just recently, I experienced a season of discouragement. I wondered if anyone really needed me or if anyone really cared about me. I felt lonely and as if I had no friends. I knew this was not true, but I was too weak to fight the thoughts. I was in need of someone bigger than the lies of the enemy. God began to overcome my feelings with truth in a most unusual way.

Within a two-week period, he surprised me with visits from people I thought I would never see again—people I figured had forgotten all about me. The first visit was from a couple who had taken me in and ministered to me many times during my college years. Now they reappeared in my life—twenty years later! Next came a young couple I had watched grow up from childhood and had sung over at their wedding. They came walking into a worship service, taking me and my heart by surprise! The very next Sunday, another couple, whom God had sovereignly brought into my life and whom he had moved away suddenly, joined us in worship. How much my God must love me to take the time to surprise me over and over again like this. How much delight he must take in lavishing his love upon us. And, oh, how often we miss his little surprises because we only see from our limited perspective—we don't see the view from his heart.

I may not see him or feel him every step of the way, but he is there. Even through the hard times—darkness all around me—he comes shining showing the way. He is like the dawn—after a long, hard night of despair—chasing all the darkness away and replacing hopelessness and sorrow with promise and joy.

Just when I think I have him figured out, he presents me with yet another gift. As I unwrap the gift—perhaps even a gift of sorrow or adversity—I am astounded to see that *he* is inside the gift and that he is revealing another little glimpse of who he is.

What a life! Every day is like a birthday party, full of twists and turns that always lead to one place—the majesty and glory of Almighty God!

M E D I T A T I O N

- What hard or sorrowful circumstances are you facing right now?

- Do you feel overwhelmed, or do you anticipate what God desires to reveal of himself through this difficulty?

- Look back over the last week. Are there any trials you faced then that you can look back upon now and say, "Oh, that is what God was doing"?

- What view from his heart has he shown you? How does this affect your outlook on life?

- How does this affect your ministry to others?

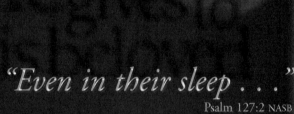

"Even in their sleep . . ."

Psalm 127:2 NASB

As you sleep tonight, ask God to give you insight into his purpose in your adversities. Trust him to give you the grace, the strength, to face any situation. Rest in knowing that he will meet you with what you need when you need it.

crown
him!

Crown Him

There is only one who will never leave you.
There is only one who can really redeem.
There is only one God who is a Savior.
There is only one who can make a heart clean.
There is only one who shines through the darkness,
Only one risen to reign.
There is only one who has crushed sin's hardness—
Jesus is his name!

Crown him! Crown him!
Jesus Christ is King!
Reigning in power!
Reigning in glory!
Reign in majesty!
Crown him! Crown him!
Jesus Christ is King!
Reigning in power!
Reigning in glory!
Reign in me! Reign in me!
Reign in me!

There is only one who could be so holy.
There is only one who can set a heart free.
There is only one who can really know me.
There is only one who can make the blind see.
There is only one God that I bow down to,
Holy and righteous is he.

There is only one who bore the Cross, shed his blood—
He is King of Kings!

INSPIRATION

Psalm 93:1–2; Hebrews 2:7–9
December 16, 1995

During the month of December 1995, the Lord provided a new piano for me and my family—a small grand piano! For years I had dreamed of having such a piano in my living room—and now my dream had come true.

Melinda and I had a grand piano when we were first married, but because of financial needs and because we needed the space for children, we had to sell it. Yet, now, God had provided! The song "Crown Him" was the first I received on this new instrument.

It came as I focused on God's goodness and on who he is to me. I knew right away that this was also a song for our little church in Muskogee—New Community Church. It became a reminder of who God has called us to be as a body—worshipers—and what he has called us to do—crown Jesus Christ as King of our lives!

Trust is simply a steadfast reliance on the integrity, ability, or character of another.

Trust in the Lord forever, for the Lord,
the Lord, is the Rock eternal.

Isaiah 26:4

There Is Only One

I once had a border collie we called Tillie. Tillie was special because she had been given to us by our Aunt Marie. We drove hundreds of miles to get her at my aunt's farm, and we enjoyed this little dog very much. Tillie was a cuddler and lavished us with wet doggie kisses. She joined us in play and even helped us round up the milk cows each night.

But our time with Tillie was short-lived. One day she was hit by a car and deeply wounded. It broke my heart to see my precious dog in such pain. My hope was shattered when each time I tried to approach her—to simply hold and comfort her—she snapped and growled at me, baring her teeth in a menacing display. She was trying to protect herself. Mortally wounded, not allowing us to minister to her, Tillie could not be helped.

Trusting another means risking a valuable part of ourselves—and this can be a dangerous thing. When we open ourselves up to others, we remove our protective layers and our hearts are exposed. Opening our hearts and disclosing our identity to others leave the heart vulnerable to wounding. And if that trust is betrayed—and we are wounded—we are less likely to risk trusting again. If such wounds are left untouched by a healing hand, our hearts tend to come to a place where trust is not worth the risk.

How many believers out there have been wounded so often they cannot receive healing, helping hands for fear of being wounded all over again? I have been there. I still battle the fear in many ways. Yet, there came a day when I had to allow someone to help me. A broken heart has to be healed by a Great Physician. As providence would have it, that Great Physician most often takes the form of human hands. God delights in using his Body to minister healing to its various parts. Why, sometimes he even uses the hands that have done the wounding to be a part of the healing.

Hearts that allow the woundings of life—the moments of broken trust and broken hearts—to draw them to Jesus find the ultimate fulfillment of trust. Trust in anything other than Jesus brings no prospect for lasting health.

Because I was a guy who played the piano, I was labeled a "sissy" and was constantly ridiculed. Thus, I grew up feeling like an outcast much of the time, and I longed for the day when I could actually be friends with someone I could share my hurts with. I especially craved and needed the approval and acceptance of other guys.

When I got to college, I found several who filled that role for me. As the Lord would have it, I became very close to three seniors during my junior year. We spent much time together because of a common position we held. I felt so blessed to be able to spend any time with them, because I felt valued and validated when I was with them. Even though they were seniors, I felt sure that our relationship would transcend any separation graduation might bring.

Boy, was I wrong! Never heard from them again! Never mind that my "parasitic" behavior probably drove them away. All I could feel was abandonment and betrayal. I had trusted them with my heart and devotion, and now they were gone.

I became so depressed and so overcome with feelings of worthlessness that I gave in to perverse depths of temptation. I sought to meet my needs for acceptance from other men in perverse ways. My downward spiral lasted for over a year and culminated with a desire to end my own life. My trust had been shattered—not because trust is a bad thing—but because I had placed it in the wrong things.

Because of sin, we let one another down from time to time. That is what forgiveness is for. But there is one—and only one—who will never let us down. When I finally placed my trust in him, the power of perverseness—of sin—was broken in my life.

Jesus Christ became to me a refuge . . .

> where I could be safe,
>
> where I could find sustenance and fulfillment,
>
> where I could abide and find rest.

He became the place . . .

> where I could unload my burdens and my frailties,

where I could be honest without fear of rejection,

where I could discover the reason I had even been created,

where I could realize my wildest dreams and true identity.

To trust, one must love. To love, one must risk being wounded. Wounding may mean being abandoned by someone I trust. Wounding may mean that my inner "secrets," once held secure by a trusted friend, are suddenly disclosed to others. On the surface, wounding may seem a tragic or hopeless state. But at its heart, wounding can be an opportunity to practice placing our trust where it does the most good—in the strong arms of a Savior. Trust became personified to me in the form of a Savior—Jesus Christ.

Like my wounded and dying dog, Tillie, I could have refused the healing touch of the one who loved me. How thankful I am that I did not. Jesus kept loving me and calling to me even when I feared trusting him. The day I finally gave my wounded heart to him was the day my wounds began to heal.

Though having one's wounds healed may require radical surgery, the healing process is worth the pain. The bandages of good intentions and "warm fuzzies" only cover the wound. For healing to take place, the wound must be cleansed and assessed by a surgeon. The surgeon cannot operate if he is never given access to the wound. Such surgery may result in scars, but the scars left by a healing hand become reminders of the surgeon's power and trophies to his skill and care. God is such a surgeon; he is one we can trust our hearts to.

The rewards of trust are priceless—peace, joy, fulfillment—things money cannot buy, things I cannot gain by my performance. The pathway of trust is founded on the bedrock of love. Trust is simply a steadfast reliance on the integrity, ability, or character of another. For me, to trust God is to commit my hopes, my dreams, my life, my fears, my hurts, my anxieties, and all that I am into his care—under his charge.

In a sense, trust is like a mighty fortress where I can find shelter, sustenance, and constant protection. Such a fortress becomes more than something I hope in. Such a fortress becomes the personification of trust. To place my life into the shelter of God is to live in trust . . . to abide in trust . . . and to have relationship with that trust.

God is such a fortress. Trust in him not only brings *him* glory, it becomes *my* glory! As I crown him the one I trust with my life, he crowns me with all he is.

He is my trust.

MEDITATION

- Has there ever been a time in your life where you have been let down by another?

- How did this make you feel? Have you been able to deal with that issue?

- What are some things you find difficult to trust to Jesus?

- Are there any wounds you would like healing for but are hesitant to disclose because you fear being wounded all over again?

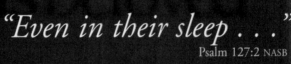

"Even in their sleep . . ."
Psalm 127:2 NASB

Ask the Lord to lead you to place your trust in him even as you dream tonight. Ask him to give you the strength to trust your hidden thoughts to him.

As his redeemed child,
I come boldly into his
presence, without fear.

For you know that it was not with perishable things
such as silver or gold that you were redeemed . . .
but with the precious blood of Christ,
a lamb without blemish or defect.

1 Peter 1:18–19

Redeemed

Men and women cannot redeem their own lives.

Redemption requires a Savior.

There is only one who can save me—only one—Jesus Christ. He had to pay my debt. He had to redeem me.

What does it mean to be redeemed? In a biblical sense, it literally means to be *bought back*. It means that Jesus Christ had to pay the purchase price for my soul—and the price was death. He took my sins upon himself and took them to the Cross. He was adequate compensation for all I owed.

In my old life—the life of sin—I was always only one heartbeat away from eternity. I was owned by Satan, and only by the grace of God was I sustained through the long dark night. Looking back, it is easy to see how foolish I really was and just how far away from the Father I had fallen. As I sought to satisfy my needs through sinful actions, I was choosing to put my very life in peril with each step into darkness I took.

I was like a lost lamb, headed for the cliff.

I was only a breath away from the hungry fangs of the wolf.

I was like a man walking a tightrope above a bottomless pit.

Each step I took was one more dance with death and a hopeless eternal destiny.

I was like a man adrift on a stormy sea.

No navigational aids. No sail. No rudder.

No idea of where I was headed, much less of how I would get there even if I knew!

I was in constant danger of being crushed to pieces upon the rocks of despair,

in constant peril of drowning in a sea of self-pity and utter hopelessness.

I was in need of someone to save me,

because I could not save myself.

I could not redeem my life: I was dead in my sin. A dead man has no power to overcome anything. A dead man requires resurrection power if he is to live. In my former state of deadness, my heart had grown so wounded and so hard that no one was able to penetrate its shell. Because I had been so wounded and because I had believed so many lies, I had built up a wall of protection around my own heart. But what was I ultimately protecting myself from? From the only one who could help me.

There came a day when I could hide no longer. I had reached the bottom of my life and desired to die a physical death. It was only then that I was able to see the extent of what Christ had really done for me upon the Cross. He had born the weight of my sin. With the first drop of his innocent blood, he had paid the insurmountable debt of my sin. Then with his death and burial came the ultimate test of God's majesty: Could he conquer death and rise again? Hallelujah! Yes! And because he was raised, now I could be raised.

I was crucified with Christ—I died with my sin nailed to his Cross and laid upon his shoulders. I was buried with Christ and then raised by the same resurrection power that he was raised to walk and reign in. He called me forth from the grave and told me to leave the old Dennis there, to follow him, and to find out who I really was called to be! The hardness of my heart had been literally crushed by the weight of his tremendous, life-changing, transforming love—never to be the same again!

Since my redemption—since my salvation—I have been blessed of the Lord to become the father of nine precious children. I have learned so much about God's character and love, as I have sought to guide, nurture, and love my own children. I used to think I could not begin to worship God or enter into his holy presence unless I was totally "confessed up." This left me always wondering if I was ever really in his presence—because I was never really sure I was totally empty of sin!

One day, one of my children fell (due to her disobedience to my commandment) and skinned her knees. She came to me crying, covered with dirt, and reaching out for me. At first I was tempted to berate her because of her disobedience, but then it occurred to me that this would have been more damaging to her little heart than the raw wounds she now suffered. At that moment, the Lord revealed to me another aspect of his majesty. When one of my children falls and becomes wounded and dirty, I do not send her away in condemnation. I do not tell her to go and cleanse herself or to bind up her own wounds. No! I take her in my arms, shine a light on the wounded place, and begin to wipe away the filth. I then bind up the wound, because I realize my child cannot do those things for herself.

This is how it is with God. When Jesus redeemed us at the Cross, we became actual sons and daughters of the Father. As redeemed children, we are never out of his presence! (Read Psalm 139.) Even when we sin, he is there calling us to turn back to him! When I fall and become dirty, I must simply come as a child to the Father, reaching out in surrender to him as the only one who can cleanse me, the only one who can bind up my wounds. As his redeemed child, I can come boldly into his presence, without fear, because I know that when he shines his light on the whole of my heart, my sin is revealed anyway! I do not fear repentance. Repentance is a gift that brings me back into that intimate place of relationship with Christ that is my hope and sustenance. His redeeming love brings healing and wholeness.

To be redeemed from my sin means to be redeemed from my past!

To be redeemed means to be rescued from eternal separation from Almighty God!

To be redeemed means that I am free, delivered, liberated!

To be redeemed means that the chains of sin that held me in bondage have been loosed!

My redemption means that the price I owed was paid—that price being the shed blood of a perfect sacrifice, Jesus Christ. And once the payment for my debt was made, I received something in exchange—a brand new life.

There is only one who can make my heart clean.

There is only one who can shine through the darkness of my life, reveal my sin, and bind up my wounds.

There is only one with that kind of love—that kind of power.

There is only one who can really redeem.

Jesus is his name!

M E D I T A T I O N

- What have you been redeemed from?
- What does it mean for you to approach God as a little child?
- When do you feel the most clean spiritually?
- Are there any hardened areas of your life you would like God to break through?

"Even in their sleep . . ."

Psalm 127:2 NASB

Ask the Holy Spirit to visit you in your dreams and remind you of what your redemption really means.

With his life, he has crowned mine. With my life, I must crown his!

There is but one Lord, Jesus Christ,
through whom all things came
and through whom we live.
1 Corinthians 8:6

Crown Him!

Jesus Christ is Lord and King of all—whether I ever acknowledge him as such or not.

In my stubbornness or in my lack of understanding, I may miss an opportunity to crown him King and Ruler in and over my life. To do so is to miss out on the inherent rewards that come from simply being the subject of the Most High King. In other words, he is King no matter what. If I want to be a part of the celebration that surrounds the King, I must acknowledge his kingship! But how do I do that?

To crown him King means enthroning him upon my heart. It means that I reserve the first and highest place of honor in my heart for the King. That is his place; it belongs to no other. By crowning him Lord and King of my life, I surrender the guardianship of my life to him.

Surrendering to him does not mean that I become a non-thinking zombie.

Surrender to him means freedom from my own frailties and access to his power.

Surrender to him means that my battles (whether mental, physical, or spiritual) become his battles—and he is jealous for his subjects!

Surrender to him means the joy of knowing that he has reserved a special place in his heart—for me—and that place in his heart belongs to me and to no other!

To crown him King means esteeming him with honor and respect. If I were to enter a room where a church fellowship was taking place, I would scarcely cause a stir to anyone but close friends. But if Billy Graham were to walk in, every head would turn and a reverent hush would permeate the atmosphere. Why? Because Billy Graham has earned a high place of esteem and honor because of the integrity he has walked in over the course of his life. He has led so many people to Jesus and poured out his life without thought for his own in such a way that even those in the secular world take notice and show deep respect when he is around. That is a good picture of what it means to crown another with esteem or respect—to honor their worth.

To crown him King means thanking him for all he has done for me. Gratitude fills my heart when I think about how he so faithfully waited for me when I ran from him in years gone by. When I enter his presence, I kneel before the King and honor him for his longsuffering love. I shower him with the epithets due a lofty person of rank or nobility. I express my high esteem and reverent respect for the one who, by his own shed blood, has saved my life. He is worthy of all my appreciation. He is a Lord who rules in power and in love, esteeming me more than I can ever esteem him!

To crown him King means acknowledging that my very existence is a result of his royal decree! He spoke me into existence! He commanded, and it was so. Nothing more. Nothing less. To acknowledge this truth is to give him the highest place of honor. To accept and walk in this truth is to crown him King of my life.

To crown him King means being crowned with his stamp of approval. With his life, he has crowned mine. With my life, I must crown his! When a building endeavor is about to be completed by one last task, the architect might say, "This will be the crowning touch." Or once that task is completed, he may stand back proudly and say, "This is my crowning achievement!" The more I seek to crown him King in my life, the more I see and understand that the deeper reality is that he has chosen to crown me with his royal stamp of approval. I cannot help but be reminded that I am his workmanship, created for good works in him—created for his pleasure—I am his crowning achievement! To be born again in Christ—to become a brand new creation—is to be brought to a successful conclusion. And then at a deeper level of completion, I look forward to the day when I am presented to the King as his pure and spotless Bride and my relationship with him is consummated—his crowning achievement!

To crown him King means sharing in his power, glory, and majesty. I am his royal child—a child of the King, created in his image, sent forth to do his bidding, sent forth to lead others to know him as I have come to know him. As a child of the King, I am endowed with his power, his glory, his majesty. Amazing!

The *power* that raised him from the dead

is the same power that rescued me and raised me from my formerly dead state of existence.

The *glory* to which he was raised

is the same glory I share by having God's presence in my life. My glory is the fact that the King of the universe rests upon me with the weight of all that he is. I am his glory and he is mine!

The *majesty* that parted the Red Sea, that shines as the Light of the world, that is declared by the heavens,

is the same majesty that now sits enthroned upon my own heart!

He is the King who rules and reigns—in my heart! His majesty now rules over and abides within my heart—seated and ruling from that special throne he himself fashioned there by his mercy and grace toward me.

He is the King who reserves a special place for me—in his heart! How can I not love him? How can I not declare his royalty? How can I not acknowledge and proclaim who he is by the way I live my life?

I will crown him. He is King!

MEDITATION

- In what areas does Christ reign freely in your life?
- Are there any areas of your life you have not given him full, royal access to?
- What crowns do you wear that rightly belong to the Lord?
- If you were planning a coronation for Jesus Christ, what would it look like in this life?
- What does it mean to you to be a child of the King?

"Even in their sleep . . ."

Psalm 127:2 NASB

Ask the King to show you your place in his kingdom—as one of his children—even as you sleep.

I cannot make myself holy.
It takes the cleansing power
of the blood of Jesus Christ
to do that.

We have been made holy
through the sacrifice of the body
of Jesus Christ once for all.

Hebrews 10:10

To Be Holy

When I think of holiness, I generally have two different pictures in my mind. One is that of a pure and perfect God. The other is that of a person who lives by a rigid set of rules— trying to gain acceptance and approval from that pure and perfect God.

God's holiness, or perfection, gives him sovereign power— unrivaled in the universe. When the payment for our sin-debt demanded perfection, only God, in the form of Jesus Christ, fulfilled the requirement. In Jesus, God painted a picture of holiness that we humans could understand.

The holiness sought by people who try to live according to a rigid set of rules is based on performance. People who seek holiness through performance often get caught up in comparing degrees of holiness and measuring their holiness by the holiness or performance of others. This tends to produce an arrogant heart and, I am sad to say, involves everyone at some point in their lives. Furthermore, their efforts are ineffective.

True holiness, or purity, cannot be measured by comparing one person's performance to another's. No. We are measured by a higher standard—the standard of God's holiness—and we have all fallen far short. We are all like sheep, each gone astray, and we are all on equal ground—each in need of a Savior. One sin does the trick. I cannot produce holiness by my performance anymore than I can create eternal life for myself. Only a perfect, powerful, pure and holy God can do that.

Holiness, like salvation, is a sovereign act of God. I cannot make myself holy. It takes the cleansing power of the blood of Jesus Christ to do that. The only act required of me is the act of receiving what is offered as a free gift. At this point, holiness takes a whole new direction. When God, through his action, makes me holy, he simultaneously dedicates and devotes me to a purpose designated by him. From the time of my salvation, I was called to be a vessel, or conduit, for God's holy and pure purposes in this life. Not only was I dedicated and designated for a holy purpose and use, I was set aside as the sole possession of the most holy person of God Almighty—set aside for God's use, chosen by the hand of God to walk in holiness with him. I am now holy in my new nature; I have a new way of thinking and a brand new identity.

To be chosen is an awesome thing. We can all probably remember times on the playground as children when teams were chosen—and how it felt to be passed over. Yet, even when continuously passed over, there always came the time when you were the only one left standing, and they had to choose you. To be chosen, even then, was an exhilarating feeling—because at least you were chosen!

Thanks be to God, we do not have to stand around waiting to be chosen! When he calls us to himself and we answer the call of grace unto salvation, the choice to be chosen becomes ours! To be chosen, personally by the Most Holy Creator of the universe, is a precious thing. There was only one who could make this possible— Jesus Christ.

> Holiness, like salvation, is a sovereign act of God.

Just as I could not make myself holy, I could not set myself free from sin in the first place. For many years, I was blinded by my own selfishness in regard to being set free. I thought I knew what I needed, yet I failed miserably each and every time I sought to meet my needs apart from God. It took the light of God's holiness to make me see; it took the mighty hand of a redeemer to break the chains that held me captive.

For years, I craved a relationship with someone who would keep loving me even if I revealed the dark, painful depths of my heart. I never felt that kind of intimacy with another human until the day I came to that place of intimacy with my God. To suddenly realize that God had been aware of all I had kept hidden—and that he loved me anyway—was the most joyous day of my life! I could be free, indeed, if I could honestly unload my heart of the years and years of burdens I had carried. I could not only know God—but I could be known by him!

It is difficult to describe how that feels on a human level. I came close a few years ago when I found myself face to face with one of those spiritual giants I had admired from afar. Jack Hayford and I had been asked to take part in a conference. I assumed we would never meet, as I was a lowly musical guest and he was a keynote speaker. Yet, I found myself sitting next to him. When he introduced himself as Jack Hayford, I responded with a demure, "I know." When I mentioned my own name, I noticed a slight moment of hesitation—as if he somehow knew my name. As we talked, he realized that his church had used one of my songs as a rallying point during a certain period in their church history. In other words, Jack Hayford was saying, "Yes, Dennis Jernigan, I know you!" One of my heroes actually had some knowledge of my feeble existence! How fulfilling and satisfying. That is how I felt when I realized that God knows me—and that he loves me anyway!

If I try to attain holiness through my own efforts, it is like placing my own heart on the throne and relegating God to the position of a lowly servant, whom I call for only when I need something. Fleshly efforts at holiness crumble and fall. Only a holy God, by an act of his sovereign will, can make me holy; only a holy God is worthy of reigning on the throne of my heart.

There is only one who is capable of such holiness.
In the light of his glory, I am quickly brought
from a selfish stance to a humble bow.
There is only one who was holy and righteous
enough to purchase my redemption.
He is the only one I can afford to bow down to.
There is only one holy enough to bear the Cross,
only one holy enough to shed his blood.
And he is King of Kings.

He is holy, and he has made me holy. He has set me apart for himself. To be chosen by God and set apart just for him is a holy calling, an honorable calling—and a good place to be if I desire to know God and to be known by him.

Holy is the Lord!

MEDITATION

- How does it make you feel to know you were chosen by God?

- What are some of the things you can see that God has set you apart for?

- Do you struggle with comparing your life to others?

- What are the idols in your life?
- What must you do to tear them down?

"Even in their sleep . . ."

Psalm 127:2 NASB

As you sleep, meditate on what it means to be chosen by God and called according to his purposes.

the rhythm of life

The Rhythm of Life

I have found the rhythm,
Felt the beat of living,
Played by one who's given me love
To the rhythm of grace!
When my heart is strayin'
From the beat he's playin',
He comes gently swayin' me back
To the rhythm of grace!

Rockin' me over the stormy sea,
Marching to the rhythm of grace—
Finding peace and security!
Really the Rhythm found me!
Never out of sync, always right on time.
Singing me through with your melody,
Never late and never behind!
You are my Rhythm and Rhyme!
You are the Rhythm of Life!

Like love set to percussion,
A musical discussion,
Steady, never rushin',
As constant as night is to day!
More than just a notion—
Poetry in motion,
Like waves upon the ocean,
Your love comes to take me away!

I have heard your rhythm
In the falling rain,
Telling me that you have
Washed away sin's stain!

I have heard your rhythm
In the flowing stream,
Telling me that you completely
Washed me clean!

INSPIRATION

Psalm 16:7–11; Matthew 11:28–30
May 30, 1996

I often go through "trying" times right before a song is given. After a particularly difficult period of back-to-back ministry times, I began to feel used up and poured out—empty. On top of my weariness came the lie that I was not needed. (The enemy often throws lies our way during times of weakness in an effort to get us to fall.) Another lie that soon followed was that no one appreciated me.

But our amazing Father God used Satan's lies for my good—he used them to reveal my self-pity and pride . . . and the fact that I need his grace more than ever. Our awesome God has a way of tying the trials and the joys into one seamless act of love and nurture, and that is what he did with my weakness and the gift of this song. The following Scripture from The Message (a new translation of the Bible by Eugene H. Peterson) was the catalyst for the phrase "rhythm of grace" in this song.

> Are you tired? Worn out? Burned out on religion? Come to me. Get away with me and you'll recover your life. I'll show you how to take a real rest. Walk with me and work with me—watch how I do it. Learn the unforced rhythms of grace. I won't lay anything heavy or ill-fitting on you. Keep company with me and you'll learn to live freely and lightly. (Matt. 11:28–30 THE MESSAGE)

As I meditated on my need for God's grace in the musical context of rhythm, this song was born!

111

Just as rhythm moves music forward, so God gives the universe its forward motion!

He will take great delight in you . . .
he will rejoice over you with singing.
Zephaniah 3:17

Rhythm

What majesty fills my heart whenever I take time to listen for the songs my Father sings over me!

When I think of the things that bring God the greatest glory and help us reflect his majesty, I think of music. I know of nothing else that commands our whole identity's attention as does music. Music involves us physically, for we sing with our bodies. Music engages us mentally, as we think about the content of the lyrics. Music affects us emotionally, as we respond to the music's rises and falls. Music touches us spiritually, if we choose to use the music to extend our hearts to the center of God's. Music envelops the senses and is a vehicle of God's grace.

After all, Paul instructed the Colossians to encourage one another with psalms, hymns, and spiritual songs. God himself tells us he will surround us with songs of deliverance (Ps. 32:7). And my favorite reference to music in God's Word tells us that he will rejoice over us with singing! (Zeph. 3:17). Following is my own translation from the Hebrew, which God has used to profoundly impact my life:

> The eternal self-existent God, the God who is three in one; he who dwells in the center of your being is a powerful and valiant warrior.
>
> He has come to set you free, to keep you safe, and to bring you victory.
>
> He is cheered, and he beams with exceeding joy and takes pleasure in your presence.
>
> He has engraved a place for himself in you, and there he quietly rests in his love and affection for you.
>
> He cannot contain himself at the thought of you and with the greatest of joy spins around wildly in anticipation over you. . . .
>
> He has placed you above all other creations and in the highest place in his priorities.
>
> In fact, he shouts and sings in triumph, joyfully proclaiming the gladness of his heart in a song of rejoicing!
>
> All because of you!
>
> (Zeph. 3:17, Translation by Dennis Jernigan)

God is the Maker of Music! He is the Singer to end all singers! Music is just one of the ways—my very *favorite* way—that God communicates with his children. Just as little babies learn to babble and then speak coherently by simply listening to what their parents say and then speaking what they hear, so we, as God's children, learn musical communication from the one who created it. When we try to convey God's majesty—his expansiveness—the power of music becomes a great communicator. How does God communicate musically?

Many different elements make up the medium we call music; but for this, and the next two devotionals, we will focus on the three main ingredients: rhythm, harmony, and melody.

Rhythm gives music its forward motion. Rhythm is a regular pattern made up of a series of notes, with each note having its own duration and emphasis. If God the Father is a rhythmic being (and I believe he is), then he will operate in the same way he has established rhythm to work. Just as rhythm moves music forward, so God gives the universe its forward motion!

Rhythm, to function properly, must follow a precise order. If it doesn't, chaos results, and God is a God of order—not chaos. We need look only as far as our own bodies to see how intricate and precise his order is. The fact that one cell from a woman and one from a man combine to create a whole new life, with all the inherent qualities and systems that life requires, testifies to his precision. A casual glance toward the heavens confirms that someone put this whole thing together. In order for life to flourish on earth, all the planets had to be aligned perfectly around the sun of our solar system. For such a massive system to operate, order had to reign supreme.

Because of God's perfect rhythm in creation, the whole universe sings the same song—a song of majesty.

God's majestic rhythm is seen most wondrously in the rhythm of *grace*. In the form of his Son, Jesus Christ, God sent out his song of salvation to all of humankind. And this beautiful, rhythmic grace is what gives our lives forward motion. Without grace, we would have no momentum—no hope. God sent his rhythm of grace into the world, searching for all who would listen and sing along.

Each time another sinner sings the song of redemption, the majestic rhythm of God is displayed!

MEDITATION

- Does your life feel in rhythm with the beat of God's heart?

- What areas of your life are out of sync with God's order?

- Do you have the ability to change rhythms in mid-song, or do you feel out of control when life throws you a different beat?

He gives to his beloved

"Even in their sleep . . ."

Psalm 127:2 NASB

Ask the Lord to allow you to experience the rhythm of his grace as you rest in his presence. Specifically, ask him to intervene in an area of your life that is out of sync.

When Jesus is allowed to conduct the symphony, disharmony gives way to harmony.

I in them and you in me.
May they be brought to complete unity
to let the world know that you sent me
and have loved them even as you have loved me.
John 17:23

Harmony

Simply stated, *harmony* is the relationship between notes when they are played at the same time. Whenever the relationship between several notes is in order and is pleasing to the ear, we say those notes are in "harmony."

Just as Father God brings *rhythm* and *order* to our lives, Jesus brings *unity*—and he brings it in several ways. First, and foundational to all spiritual harmony, is the eternal harmony Jesus *brought between us and the Father* when he bridged the gap of sin through his death on the Cross. Without the blood of Jesus to cleanse and bring us into fellowship with the Father, we would never know harmony, or peace, with God.

Christ also brings harmony to the *Body of Christ.* Think of each part of the Body of Christ as a separate musical note. When those notes operate in proper harmonic order, we have harmony, or unity. Whenever those notes cannot agree, we have a lack of harmony, or discord. God's majesty is no greater than when all of God's children choose to live God's harmony as they relate to one another!

One of the saddest commentaries against Christianity today is the lack of harmony in the Body of Christ. God's Word tells us plainly that the world will know we are Christians by our love. Harmony, I believe, is a by-product of love. If we say we have the love of God abiding in us but do not have love for one another, then God's Word is very clear: we are nothing more than noisy, clanging gongs.

You know what a gong is, don't you? A gong is like a cymbal—an instrument of rhythm. When a gong is played in the proper rhythm, in the proper order, and with the proper measure of pressure, it is a beautiful, pleasing addition to the symphony. But when a gong is played just to gain attention or to be heard, it is considered rude, ugly, and offensive. When we feel inadequate or insecure in our identity—when we do not rest in our place and operate in the function in which Father God

> Harmony with Christ is simply learning to sing your part—your heart—with his!

intended—we tend to be more like the noisy gong than the pleasing instrument. When this occurs, we need a deeper understanding of the work of Christ's redemption in our lives. In other words, when I feel unloved or unneeded, I may play my gong to gain attention. But if I rest in the fact that I am totally accepted in the Body of Christ and the heart of God, by virtue of the shed blood of Christ, then I am a pleasing instrument. We all play the noisy gong from time to time— and that is not necessarily a bad thing. How can we understand and enjoy the nature of harmony if we never experience the pain of disharmony?

Finally, the harmony of Christ brings unity and peace to our *personal lives.* Life, because of sin, is full of disharmony. But when Jesus is allowed to conduct the symphony, disharmony gives way to harmony. When trials come and we feel like giving up, we have a choice to make. Will we listen for and respond to the harmony of Christ, or will we listen to and respond to the chaos of the lies the enemy tries to sing to our minds?

My own personal story (redemption from homosexuality) brings this aspect of harmony to life in a vivid way for me. For years, I tried to work my way into freedom. I tried to perform for God's approval and acceptance—when I had it through Jesus all along. The very things I feared—rejection, abandonment, and aloneness—became the harmonic melodies of my life when sung by Jesus. But only when my pathetic song of self-reliance ground to an ugly halt was I able to hear the harmony of Jesus—a beautiful song of sorrow played upon the shoulders of the one who bore my sin. I heard him singing his love and acceptance to me. I heard him sing things like:

Come out from the tomb, Dennis; leave the old
Dennis there.

I have made you into someone brand new.

Come out here with me and learn of me.

Let me teach you the song of reality—the song
of truth, freedom, and life.

Pretty cool song, huh?

When I finally accepted the freedom Christ offered
me . . .

the chains of sin began to fall away from my
heart and life.

When I began to hear his songs of love . . .

hope was restored to me and my life began to
operate in harmony with the heart of
Christ.

If he sings of hope, love, and grace,

then so will I.

If he sings freedom to the captives and healing to the
brokenhearted,

then so will I.

If he sings the harmonies of liberty and acceptance,

then so will I.

Harmony with Christ is simply learning to sing your
part—your heart—with his!

MEDITATION

- In what areas of your life do you sense disharmony?
- In what relationships (God, family, friends) do you sense a lack of harmony?
- What is God's perspective on the disharmonies of your life?
- What changes need to occur in your heart to bring harmony to your life?

"Even in their sleep . . ."

Psalm 127:2 NASB

As you sleep, ask the Lord Jesus to bring harmony and peace to every thought, that you might awaken refreshed by the peace of his harmony.

What had begun as a
sad and sorrowful
melody from my soul
was rearranged by the
Master Musician
into a matchless melody.

You have made known to me the path of life;
you will fill me with joy in your presence.

Psalm16:11

⚜

Melody

A *melody* is a series of notes that are rhythmically organized into an expression of music that is easily remembered and recognized. This is what the Holy Spirit brings to our lives—he rhythmically organizes the events of our lives into a *melodic symphony* of praise to his majesty.

In the New Testament, the word for the Holy Spirit comes from the Greek word for "breath." In other words, the Holy Spirit is the very breath of God, and he brings the breath of life to us! In the physical realm, where does the power to produce sound—speaking and singing—come from? It comes from the breath. As believers, where does our power to live life melodiously come from? It comes from the Breath of God—the Holy Spirit! When we walk in the power of the Holy Spirit, our lives will be melodic—even when storms come.

In fact, the storms of life are lovingly arranged by the Spirit to become vital components of a beautiful melody. God's grace—through the power of the Holy Spirit—tends to arrive just when we need it and in just the right amount. This truth was made vividly real to my family when my wife, Melinda, gave birth to our twin sons, Asa and Ezra. Her body developed toxemia, which, in turn, led to liver damage. Our physician ordered an ultrasound, and our suspicions were confirmed. Melinda's liver had been bruised due to her high blood pressure and the trauma of labor. The doctor very calmly explained that this was a life and death situation and that surgery was not the best option. She said that if we were praying people, this was the time to pray.

After the doctor left the room, I simply sat there in the dark and cried. I had no prayers left in me. I was all "prayed out" after praying over the babies (who were born nine

> Even the storms of life are lovingly arranged by the Holy Spirit as vital components of a beautiful melody.

weeks prematurely). It was as if I were watching Melinda being swept along by a powerful current toward a treacherous waterfall, and there was nothing I could do! I felt helpless and useless—a man of prayer now unable to pray! Finally, I released her to the Lord and came to peace with whatever his will was.

It was then that he whispered to my heart and assured me that he heard my cries and saved my tears. I did not understand why the Lord would want to save my tears, but I was somehow comforted. Still unable to pray, I continued to quietly release my tears.

After a few minutes, Melinda asked me to leave the room to cry! During my absence, Melinda told the Lord she was ready to be in his presence. But do you know what he said to her? He said, "No, Melinda. I will come and be in your presence." This statement was to carry her through her whole ordeal.

Even though I felt I was losing my wife, I felt a certain peace that is difficult to adequately explain. I just knew God's presence was with me. I was not alone. Melinda was not alone. God, by the presence and power of the Holy Spirit, was orchestrating the melody of our lives—he was with us! Because of Melinda's dire situation, I knew I needed to call her mother (who lived several states away) and apprise her of what was going on. After the phone call, I walked down the hall and was met by a nurse who pulled me aside. She told me she had not been scheduled to work that evening, but had been called in at the last minute— and now she knew why! She had been called in for me and Melinda! She assured me that others were taking up the prayer battle in my weakness

. . . and then she shared that God wanted me to know that he was saving my tears and that he heard them as the prayer of my heart. Now, I understood why he was saving my tears! He was hearing them as the prayers I could not articulate. Thank you, Lord!

The very thing I felt inadequate to do, God supplied, by the power of the Holy Spirit. He orchestrated that night's symphony in such a way that I could not miss his presence! What had begun as a sad and sorrowful melody from my soul was rearranged by the Master Musician into a matchless melody so exquisitely marked with God's authorship that we could only give him glory.

The melody we sing, when released to him, becomes a symphony of praise to the power and majesty of a God so big that he is unfathomable, yet so genuinely interested and acquainted with his children that he takes delight in interacting on the most intimate levels of relationship with us.

To make music with God—to seek to know him—is to walk intimately in *relationship* with him. How open and honest we are with him will determine how deeply he can affect and orchestrate our lives.

His melody is sweet and consistent,
always playing whether we face storms or peaceful calm.
His melody is most often expressed in the lives of those instruments
he can breath through!
His melody is life and freedom,
born on the breath of grace.

MEDITATION

- If your life was a melody, what would that melody sound like?
- Have you ever felt the presence of the Lord? What did it feel like?
- What situation are you currently facing where you need the power of the Holy Spirit?
- What things or attitudes do you need to surrender in order to receive his grace, his power?
- What do you think the melody of God's heart sounds like?

"Even in their sleep . . ."
Psalm 127:2 NASB

As you rest, allow the Holy Spirit to sing over the fears, anxieties, or concerns of your life. Ask him to wash your heart with the melodies of grace so that your soul and body will awake refreshed and looking forward to experiencing more of his grace!

SIX

I was created
to love you

I Was Created
to Love You

Oh, how I love thinkin' of you, because I love you.
For I was created to love you, and I love you.
But Lord, more of your presence, I can't contain it,
For you overflow my heart—so deepen my heart
For loving you more every day than I did at the start!

For I was created to love you
Even before time began.
You fill my heart with your pleasure,
For I was created to love you,
And, Lord, I do!

I won't pretend to explain it, the way I love you.
My heart can't begin to contain it; I simply love you.
For I know just how hopeless my life was without you,
Until you drew me to your heart, so here is my heart
For loving you more every day than I did at the start!

I love you. I love you. I love you.
For I was created to love you, and, Lord, I do!

INSPIRATION

Psalm 8; Colossians 1:16
July 6, 1987

One day as I sat at the piano thinking about the ways God has displayed his love toward me, I was overwhelmed with the thought that he created me just for himself. In other words, I was literally created to love him and to be with him and to know him intimately.

Sometimes, my feeble little mind can only contain so much of this truth without feeling totally dumbfounded and incapable of rational thought—his thoughts are so much higher than mine, his ways so much more magnificent than mine, his love for me so much greater than my love for him. I was created to love him!

"It is time that you stepped out of the nest and learned to rely on your own wings of faith."

We are God's workmanship,
created in Christ Jesus to do good works,
which God prepared in advance
for us to do.
Ephesians 2:10

I Was Created
to Love God

The workmanship of God—that is what I am.

One of my favorite things to do is to meditate on how much God loves me. Inevitably, this brings me to the place of gratitude and leaves me caught up in expressing my love to him. It seems to me, sometimes, that my sole purpose in life is to simply express my love to him—but then things like work and responsibility bring me back into reality! But is that really reality?

When I look at the people around me, I see many wonderful giftings and talents. Some are natural givers—benevolent and generous. Some are natural servants—gracious and selfless. Some are natural musicians—playing or singing and bringing great joy and comfort to the hearts of men and women. Some are natural artists—capturing on canvass a picture that instantly transports those who see it to the very instant it was created.

Still others seem naturally gifted in a corporate setting—wheeling and dealing as if they had been created for such a purpose. Others seem just as naturally gifted in a blue-collar setting— hands on at the construction sight. I know physicians who seem created for just exactly what they do. I see nurses and other care-givers whose gifts seem to flow from some unseen pool of resources that turns them into ministering machines! If we simply look around, we will see majestic strokes of God's creative hands in each individual person.

It seems to me, sometimes, that my sole purpose in life is to simply express my love to him.

God's Word says that we were created in Christ Jesus for good works (Eph. 2:10). Every gifting I just mentioned involves a good work. His Word also says that all things were created *by* him and *for* him: "For by him all things were created:

things in heaven and on earth, visible and invisible, whether thrones or powers or rulers or authorities; all things were created by him and for him" (Col. 1:16). Even though we see an endless array of talents and giftings—even though some of those giftings may seem obscure or nonspiritual—all are of equal importance in God's economy. If God was willing to take the time to make each person unique, it stands to reason that he would also have a unique *purpose* for each and every one of us.

For many years I struggled with my identity. This went hand in hand with my struggle to know my purpose for even existing. I remember debating about what I would do as a profession while still in high school. Should I pursue a medical career? I felt drawn to help people who were hurting. Should I pursue the field of commercial art? I loved to draw and use those drawings to bless others. Should I pursue a basketball scholarship and play in the NBA? I loved the game and felt I had the passion to play on that level. (Okay, so some of my dreams were fantasy!) Should I pursue a ministry in the field of music? I had played piano from an early age and felt drawn to express my heart in musical form.

After much debate and the harsh reality of university life, I quickly saw that I did not have the will to face so many years of medical school. As far as my drawing, I did not see a future in it for me—there were so many people with much more talent. Besides, I could still use my artistic gift to bless others. Concerning basketball, I finally realized that something had to go—I needed to work and I had chosen a music major. So, music became the logical choice. Little did I know, this was the God-ordained path of my life!

As my college days turned into years, I had still other choices to make. Should I obtain my teaching degree rather than a purely ministerial degree? After all, a teaching certificate would be something I could fall back on if the ministry thing didn't pan out. Even as blind as I was, I chose to take the ministerial path and sought a degree in church music. It was somewhere during this time that I was introduced to the ministry of Keith Green. Having had the opportunity to sit under his ministry in 1978, I had been so inspired by his passion and so overwhelmed with the way hearing him speak made me feel that I wanted to be just like him.

After graduation, God did a great work in my life, setting me free from the bondage of sin and healing me of deep-seated wounds. I was learning my identity. Along with an inkling of who I was came the faint glimmer of understanding the calling or purpose of my life—I felt called of God to minister to others, just like Keith Green. As I sought to know God intimately, I often used the music of Keith Green. I tried to play the piano like Keith (like a gnat trying to keep up with a soaring eagle!), and I tried to sing like Keith (like a turkey trying to imitate a canary!). I was beginning to understand Paul's admonition for others to do as he did in ministry. I was simply trying to learn from Keith. My heart was broken the day Keith died. Though we had never met, I felt I knew him. It was not long before I began to feel that maybe God needed another Keith Green—and that just maybe he would use me.

But do you know what God did for me? He broke my heart to that dream . . . and gave me a better one. How could that be? He plainly and lovingly told me this: "Dennis—

son—I don't need another Keith Green. I only wanted one
. . . and he is mine. I want you to be Dennis. I need a Dennis Jernigan to express my heart and love to my children. You
have a definite destiny and a holy purpose. It is time that you
stepped out of the nest and learned to rely on your own wings
of faith. I want you."

Created by him and for him, each one of us is unique and
called to a specific purpose—no matter how we are gifted, no
matter our status in life. You were created to be you, and I was
created to be me—each created to minister the love of God
through the conduit of our own individual lives. When we
can accept this truth, and then each accept the giftings of one
another, God's creativity will know no bounds. One gift used
in combination with the next . . . and the next . . . and the
next . . . brings great glory to God and releases supernatural
power.

The reality of who you are and what your purpose in life
is, is so simple: from the lowliest, menial profession to the
grandest artistic talent, there is only one ultimate purpose for
all—and that is to bring glory to God!

MEDITATION

- Do you feel unique? Why or why not?
- Do you feel you know how God has called you specifically?
- How could God express his love for others through you
  at your workplace?

- What lies have you believed about yourself that have limited God's expression through you?

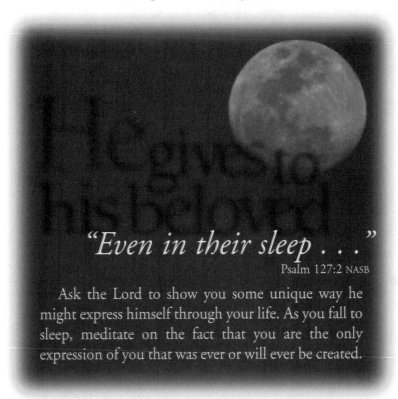

He gives to his beloved

"Even in their sleep . . ."

Psalm 127:2 NASB

Ask the Lord to show you some unique way he might express himself through your life. As you fall to sleep, meditate on the fact that you are the only expression of you that was ever or will ever be created.

The heat of this life can be scorching, but nothing quenches the thirst or alleviates the dryness like a taste of God's presence!

I spread out my hands to you;
my soul thirsts for you like a parched land.
Psalm 143:6

Deepen My Heart

After a long day of helping my dad in the hayfield, he would often take me and my brothers to Cole's Filling Station for a cool drink of soda pop. My drink of choice was always Chocolate Soldier. To me, that cold, chocolaty concoction felt like heaven going down my throat, bringing ecstasy and joy to my innermost being. I looked so forward to those treats that it became almost an obsession!

Can you remember some time in your childhood when you had the opportunity to taste something that delightful? How did it make you feel? It always left me wanting more and dreaming of the next time I would taste my Chocolate Soldier.

In the early days of my freedom from bondage, I was like that little boy of so long ago. I had finally tasted something of

God's presence, and it felt like heaven on earth. For so long I had longed to know him and to be known by him, and now that hope had become reality! Countless times I sat, literally, for hours, soaking in his presence, marveling at the ramifications of his deep love for me. It was as if I had finally gotten to taste something I had dreamed about tasting for years. And when I finally tasted it, my desire for that clean, cool, refreshing sense of his presence and love were insatiable.

Whereas before, I had craved the attention of others, I now craved the attentions of my God—and I found that I had his undivided attention. In my former state of lostness, I had sought to meet my needs through bitter waters. With each drink of sin, my spiritual well-being was set back a little further. Yet now I found myself incapable of containing all I was drinking in of God's presence.

I have come to realize that who God has created me to be—a vessel for his filling and of his expression to the world—has only so much capacity. In my human form, I can only hold so much of him! Yet, because I am ultimately a spiritual being, I believe my capacity for God can be expanded. I have only touched the tip of the iceberg of who God is. At the same time, I have only touched the tip of the iceberg of who he has created me to be!

What this means is that I am in constant process: putting off the old, putting on the new. For so many years, I believed deadly lies concerning my true identity. Once God changed my identity—transforming me—I had to accept the fact that I was starting all over again, that I had to learn to crawl, then walk, then run . . . and eventually to *fly* over the cares of this life. In learning to walk as that new creation he has made me to be, I am, in essence, ever expanding my ability to perceive, believe, and receive all God is. My incredible journey has only just begun! I have eternity to know him!

Sometimes my Dad would allow me to have not one, but two Chocolate Soldiers, and I would long to be able to contain all of that soothing sweetness. And now, when I sense God's marvelous presence in my life, I long for those times to go on forever . . . yet I cannot begin to contain it all. Just as I longed for more of that soda pop, I now long for and look forward to each and every meeting . . . each and every drink of the Lord's presence in my life.

My prayer has become like the song:

> But Lord, more of your presence—I can't contain it,
>
> For you overflow my heart—so deepen my heart
>
> For loving you more every day than I did at the start!

To know him more every day, to receive more of his love every day, to express my own love for him more every day—this is my desire.

Would you like to know something amazing? The amount of pleasure I receive from those cool, refreshing drinks of the Lord's presence is nothing compared to the amount of pleasure he finds and takes in me and my presence! It's true! God takes more delight in my presence than I do in his. If you don't believe me, think about this: Do your thoughts toward him outnumber the sands of the sea as do his thoughts towards you? (Ps. 139). Do you spin around wildly in anticipation at the very thought of him as he does at the thought of you? (Zeph. 3:17).

God's Word tells us that while we were still lost in sin, Christ died for us (Rom. 5:8). Herein lies yet another mystery of his great majesty: my sin left me unworthy, yet he saw worth in me—enough worth, in fact, to compel him to forsake the joys and riches of heaven and to take my place on the Cross of crucifixion. I don't understand it. I don't have to. I simply need to receive it!

God so loved us that he gave his only Son, that whoever would believe on him would have eternal life (John 3:16). God could have simply *thought* about his love toward me, but that would not have been true love. True love is always *expressed* love. God's Word does not say that God so loved the world that he *thought* about maybe sending his only Son. No. His Word tells us that God so loved the world that he gave his only Son. Love that is not expressed is not love.

God expressed his love to me. I received that love and have been overwhelmed with it ever since! With every new level of trust I learn to walk in, I am brought to a whole new vista of the expansiveness of that love. Just when I think I know something about God, he blows my mind by taking me to places of his character or my identity that I didn't even know existed!

His love for me compels me to express my love for him all the more.

His love for me leaves me wanting more of him.

Just as, after a long, hot day in the sun of the hayfield, I longed to have my thirst quenched by those Chocolate Soldiers, I now desire to have my spiritual thirst quenched daily by his awesomely sweet presence!

The heat of this life can be scorching, but nothing quenches the thirst or alleviates the dryness like a taste of God's presence!

Deepen my heart to receive more of you, Lord!

M E D I T A T I O N

- What does God's presence "taste" like to you?

- What does it mean to thirst for the Lord?

- How does God expand the heart for receiving more of his presence?

- Are you experiencing dryness in your life? Do you feel as if you, from time to time, are stranded in a dry and weary desert? How does one's thirst get quenched in a desert?

"Even in their sleep . . ."

Psalm 127:2 NASB

Ask God to quench some thirsty area of your life
as you sleep tonight.

God decided to take a shapeless lump of clay in his hands and create a masterpiece.

O Lord, you are our Father.
We are the clay, you are the potter;
we are all the work of your hand.
Isaiah 64:8

Before Time Began

Have you ever wondered what God was doing before time as we know it began? I have!

God, being all knowing, contained every created thing in his thoughts. Being creative in nature, he took the next step in the creative process and fashioned his thoughts into tangible, expressive forms.

The word *create* means to cause something to exist that did not exist before, it means to bring that "something" into a state of being. To create can also mean producing something through artistic or imaginative effort. God did both when he created you and me.

Not only did he bring my eternal soul into existence, he exercised great care and imagination in forming every cell of my "earth-suit," in which my spirit and soul would live out their physical days. He invested great consideration and thought in creating my psychological makeup (some might even say this proves God has a sense of humor—and yes, I am inclined to agree!). He also uniquely fashioned the very core of my being—my spirit—making me the only Dennis Jernigan there ever was and ever would be. To repeat that entire creative process billions and billions of times, truly reflects the incomprehensible majesty of Almighty God.

Ephesians 2:10 says that "we are His workmanship, created in Christ Jesus for good works, which God prepared *beforehand,* that we should walk in them" (NASB, emphasis added). But before what? Before the world and time existed as we know them! That is quite a lot of forethought. To us, that kind of thought process seems impossible. To imagine "good works" for billions of individual souls, thinking of each one individually—and yet simultaneously—is mind-boggling! But that is exactly what our God is capable of doing—he thinks of each of us ceaselessly and simultaneously. What a mighty God! "How precious to me are your thoughts, O God! How vast is the sum of them! Were I to count them, they would outnumber the grains of sand" (Ps. 139:17–18).

Our God is the Master Artist. One day, God took a shapeless lump of clay in his hands and decided to create a masterpiece. Lovingly, allowing his imagination to flow, he sculpted and shaped my physical frame—just as a potter patiently works the clay—imagining my very form into being. With just the right amount of pressure and spinning, with precisely placed strokes of his gentle hand, the vessel that he would call Dennis was born. When it came time to add color to this clay canvass, he thought about all the varieties of color he had at his disposal . . . and why not? He was the one who painted those very colors into existence! Then he graciously dipped his brush into the physical realm and began to paint my life, choosing colors that would allow onlookers to know that it was his hands that had shaped, molded, and colored this precious creation.

When the vessel developed a flaw, the Potter was not discouraged. He just kept reshaping and reforming the lump of clay each time it showed some weakness. In fact, he kind of liked the character each flaw produced in the overall form.

At every point of weakness or cracking,

he lovingly applied a stroke of grace.

At every point of brittleness,

he patiently added layers of forgiveness.

At every point of darkness,

he generously applied a coating of faith.

At every point of its outer surface—

at every point below or above, at every point within the deepest recesses—

he applied the sealant of love, and this sealant

had the unique ability to permeate every hidden place and to soak deeply into every pore of the little vessel's existence.

And then he placed it in the fiery kiln of life to bring maturity and finality.

Even before time began, Father God knew exactly what I would look like . . . how I would act . . . how I would think . . . and every other thing there was to know about me. He did not stop at simply *creating* this vessel called Dennis, but he filled me with his very *presence* and made me a vessel of his creativity to this world . . . a vessel of his love to others.

This pot called Dennis learned what it means to be a "crackpot" the day he learned that God best uses broken vessels. Because of my past—my failures—I had always thought there was no way God could use me. But through his grace, I finally learned that the vessel who walks in recognition of his need and brokenness is the vessel who receives the place of honor—the honor of being used as a vessel of the King. And I learned that no matter where I find myself—whether in a fiery kiln or in the position of a lowly serving piece—that if I acknowledge my weakness and submit to the Potter's hand, the Creator will fill me to the brim with his very *presence.*

Sometimes, vessels can be full of the Lord but desire to keep that fullness for themselves. But if not disbursed to others, that filling tends to evaporate—to dry up. It is the vessel that allows itself to be broken and spilled out, releasing the fragrance of love and life to those in need, that receives the special care and attention of the Master's hand. A broken vessel in God's economy is a valuable treasure—a treasure the Master delights in filling to overflowing, again and again. This vessel realizes that allowing itself to be broken—in order to release the power that has been placed within it—is what gives the vessel its true and priceless value.

A broken vessel in the hands of a Master God is like a brush in the hand of a Master Painter. That Painter—Father God—has the palette of the riches of his kingdom at his disposal. His greatest desire is to paint a picture of Christ's heart of love and hope before all people. God had all this (and more) in mind when he thought of you before time began—all this and more.

This is your destiny, imagined in the heart of God before the foundations of this world, then spoken into existence at the exact and proper time you were needed.

What power. What love. What majesty—even before time began.

M E D I T A T I O N

- In what stage of God's creative process are you right now? Molding? Shaping? Fiery kiln? Brokenness?
- How does one get "filled" with God's presence?
- How does it make you feel to know that God wants you to be broken and spilled out?
- How was he broken and spilled out for you?

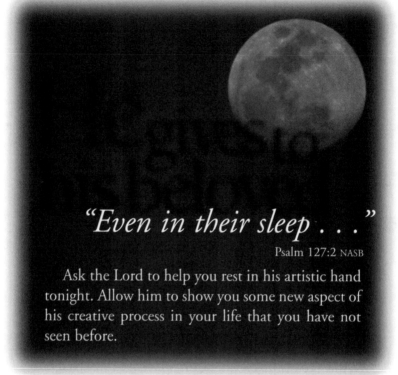

"Even in their sleep . . ."

Psalm 127:2 NASB

Ask the Lord to help you rest in his artistic hand
tonight. Allow him to show you some new aspect of
his creative process in your life that you have not
seen before.

God used my
marriage to show
me new levels of
love and its
commitment.

The only thing that counts is faith
expressing itself through love.

Galatians 5:6

How Could I Love You More?

I remember the feelings of newness and wonder the first time I saw the woman who would become my wife, as I contemplated whether she was the one for me and wondered if what I felt was love. I remember the heartache and confusion I felt as I agonized over the life-changing decision to ask her hand in marriage—to actually make such a covenant with another human being was mind-boggling. I remember the excitement I felt the day I finally proposed marriage to Melinda.

Yes, when we think of love, we most often think of feelings. But what we see demonstrated on the Cross of Christ was not a *feeling*, but an act—a commitment—of one life to another.

SIX: I WAS CREATED TO LOVE YOU

On the day Melinda and I were married, I felt nothing could dampen my love for her. But as any young married man or woman soon finds out, the feelings of love are quickly dissipated by that first disappointment when you discover that your precious princess has a little T-rex in her blood or that your knight in shining armor acts a little too much like Dr. Jekyl and Mr. Hyde! No, it doesn't take long before the real meaning of love must be explored.

I soon learned that real love has to do with commitment—with a decision to lay down my life for the one I loved—no matter what. To do anything less was not truly love.

What often kept me going in my quest to love my wife unconditionally—for better or for worse—was the picture Christ had painted for me in my own life. It was easy to remember that even though my life had been filled with sin and failure, even though I deserved no good thing, God had loved me still.

God never gave up on me . . .

    even when I gave up on myself.

He never stopped loving me . . .

    even when I did not love myself.

He never left me . . .

    even when I turned from him.

He laid down his life for me . . .

    even when I was dead in my sin.

His love was poured out

    through his commitment to me.

160

His love was made real

    as he put it into action on my behalf—no matter how I treated him.

Perfect love. Unconditional love. Endless love.

As God will do, he began to use my marriage to show me new levels of love and its commitment. In those early years, Melinda and I often found it difficult, at best, to feed our two babies on the nine hundred dollars a month I brought home as a teacher—that was my salary for nine months of the year. Those other three months were spent doing odd jobs and selling our crafts wherever we could. Many were the times we subsisted on potatoes or popcorn.

It was by God's love for us, as expressed through his majestic grace, that we did not give up—not on each other and not on him. Even though I often wondered why Melinda had ever married me—I wondered even more why she stayed with me.

I recall the time I became so angry that I put my fist through the windshield of a borrowed car. Melinda was a month pregnant with our first child at the time. If I had been Melinda, I would have left me right then and there! Though she was totally capable of taking care of herself (she had a master's degree and had already taught courses at a major university in Dallas), she demonstrated to me that day that she was committed to me for the long haul. Such a commitment was almost too good to be true. Yet, it was just such a commitment, just such a love, that carried us through some very trying times—like the day I informed her, after five years of marriage, that I had formerly been active in the homosexual lifestyle.

She didn't flinch. She didn't budge. Her response was total acceptance. She informed me, in no uncertain terms, that she was more committed to me than ever and that she was grateful I loved and trusted her enough to be honest with her. She only wished I had done it sooner! What love.

I recall the day I became angry with her for getting the van stuck in the mud. I had to leave my writing and drive a tractor from my dad's farm to ours in a pouring rainstorm! When the tractor proved too small for the job, I had to go to my brother's farm and get the big tractor. While on the way, the front end loader collapsed into the ground just as the transmission was bumped out of gear. Digging into the ground with the front end, the tractor almost flipped head over heals right on top of me. When I finally got the van out of the bottomless pit, I felt somewhat justified in my anger . . . until I began to allow the Lord to remind me of my commitment to love—no mat-

Love is a commitment that must be lived out in the harsh realities of life.

ter what. Melinda had not gotten the van stuck just to cause me heartache. Melinda had not caused the rain. Melinda had not caused tractor boy to unwittingly enter his tractor into the demolition derby. Because of my selfish attitude—thinking that everything revolved around me—I had not walked in love toward my wife. This is but one small account among countless incidents of selfishness we each experience on a day-to-day basis.

Christ never gave thought to his own life when laying it down for me, and he has called me to do that for my wife and children and others.

Love is a commitment that must be lived out in the harsh realities of life. But the fruit of love is a peace that surpasses all human understanding.

God loved me—
    I gained forgiveness.
God loved me—
    I gained a new life.
God loved me—
    my life is sustained through any trial.

What is true in loving God is true in marriage. Just when you think you can't love anymore, your capacity for love deepens.

I did not think I could love my wife more than on our wedding day . . .

then our first child was born.

I did not think I could love my wife anymore
than I did than when our first child was
born . . .

and then the next child came!

(And on and on and on to the grand total
of nine!)

I did not think I could love my wife or children anymore than when she gave birth and our
children were born . . .

and then I almost lost her and the twins.

It seems that with every trial, through every fear, through
times of failure and disappointment, through personal weaknesses and family heartaches, love is never dampened. It is as
if our hearts are stretched to contain more—they contain
more so that more may be poured out.

This is the joy of love:

knowing that God's commitment to us resulted in
life,

knowing that there is nothing we can face in life that
God will not walk us through,

knowing that life can throw nothing our way that
God cannot use to expand our hearts for
even greater depths of love.

I love God because he first loved me. My love, at times,
seems boundless. I won't pretend to explain it. My heart cannot begin to contain it. I simply love him.

How could I love him more? By knowing him in an intimate way and by resting in his love for me.

MEDITATION

- What are some of the ways God has expressed his love in your life?

- How does his love for you make you want to respond to him?

- What does the word mean to you?

- What are some of the reasons you have to be grateful for God's love?

"Even in their sleep . . ."

Psalm 127:2 NASB

Ask the Lord to remind you of some of the ways
he has loved you even when you did not love him.

you alone
are King

You Alone Are King

Lord of the heavens—Lord of the earth—
You alone give my life its worth!
Here is my heart, Lord, for you a throne,
Reserved for one King alone!

Mighty God, the Ruler of my heart!
Mighty God, my heart's true King!
You alone reign in majesty!
You alone reign in glory!
You alone! You alone!
You alone are King!

Maker of Music, make melody.
Hold me and sing over me!
Sing me your love song.
Fill me with grace.
I long to know your embrace!

INSPIRATION

Psalm 22:3; Ephesians 5:19
July 24, 1990

For so long, my life seemed worthless to me. This song was birthed as I focused on how much worth God's redemption had bestowed upon my life. The paradox here is that my sin did make me unworthy, yet God deemed me worth the life of his Son, Jesus—and Jesus felt me worth giving up the glories and riches of heaven for.

Worship is relationship, and relationship begins in the heart. God's Word says that he inhabits the praises of his people. As I meditated on this truth, I saw my heart as his throne—a place reserved for only one King—Jesus Christ. As the music began to flow from these thoughts, I realized that God was truly the author of my faith, singing his love over me. In that instant I truly felt the embrace of God and bowed in worship to my heart's true King.

No other had ever met my needs like Jesus. No one else could cleanse and heal as he can. He alone is my heart's deepest desire, and he alone is the Ruler—the King—of my heart.

He conveys his might with every bolt of lightning and every wave that crashes against the shore.

You are worthy, our Lord and God,
to receive glory and honor and power,
for you created all things,
and by your will they were created
and have their being.

Revelation 4:11

He Is Lord

Lord—the one with power and authority. Master—the one who is over all. That is who God is. He is Lord. What is there that he has not mastered? What is there that he does not have power and authority over?

I can think of nothing.

He has conquered sin.

He has conquered death.

He has the power to command life and to restore.

He has the authority to put the enemy to flight.

He has all power. He has all authority. He is Master and Lord of all!

171

Lord of the heavens. God spoke the heavens into existence. I don't understand how, but I know without a doubt that the one with all the power, the one who created it all, is its Lord. God shaped each star, and his Word tells us that he gave each a name. He fashioned every planet and set each in precise orbit. He declares his existence through the nightly display of his handiwork. Each planet depends upon the gravitational pull of another to keep it in place. Each planet depends upon the gravitational pull of the sun to keep it in motion. Each one depending upon the other—all designed with amazing forethought and with perfection of design.

This was not a chance happening.

This was no accident.

Too many coincidences for this earth-boy. God created the heavens by his power, and their glory shouts to all that there is a God—and that he is Lord.

Lord of the earth. The earth is the Lord's and all it contains. From the inner depths of its molten center to the frozen crust of the poles, God has created this earth. He spoke its form and its contents into existence and put each component in its proper place. He instilled it with human life and allowed that life to choose whether or not it would seek to know him. He made it all by the power of his Word. He proclaims his glory with every mountain peak. He conveys his might with every bolt of lightning and every wave that crashes against the shore. He displays his intricate design and purpose in the tapestry we call life. The birds of the air need water. The fish of the sea need air. The seed needs the soil in which to grow.

The soil needs the nutrients the seed and its fruit leave behind. Each part depending upon and needing the other for existence. Only one with power could have put such a complex design together.

*T*his was no accident.
No chance was involved.

It is all too precise. He has the power. He is Lord.

Lord of my heart. My human heart, from the design of its chambers to the vastness of the cardiovascular system, is a most amazing "machine"—perfect in design, awesome in function. Without its constant beating, without the ebb and flow of lifeblood, our lives—our existence in human form—could not be sustained. Yet what gives the heart the power to beat? Who tells it to pump? Is this simply an example of evolutionary chance? Is it a freak happenstance or an accident of nature? I don't think so!

Even as awe-inspiring as the complexities of the human heart are, they pale in comparison to the wonders and glories of the spiritual heart—the *essence* of who we are. My human heart is frail and finite. The core of my spirit—my heart—is an eternal entity. The core of who I am is found at the heart of my spirit. Only one with supernatural power could create such a thing.

*N*o luck or chance.
No accidents of nature.

Only one with power could create such a heart. God has the power. He is Lord—whether I believe it or not!

The spiritual heart, apart from God, is like a physical heart that does not beat. It exists, but it has no power to save itself—no power to give itself life. The only way for the heart of man to be revived is to be infused with life by the power of God.

This is no accident.

No game of chance.

Apart from God, the spiritual heart is bound for death, destruction, and hell. Humans sinned, and their spirits died. But thanks be to God, he made a way for our hearts to be restored to life through the blood of Jesus Christ.

Only one with the power to conquer sin

could revive such a dead heart.

Only one with the power to take the whole of humankind's sin upon his shoulders and be crucified to pay that debt

could offer that kind of forgiveness.

Only one with the power to conquer the grave

could restore and resurrect such a heart.

Only one with the power to invade hell and overcome death

could raise up a dead heart.

Only the Lord of the heavens—the Lord of the earth—the Lord of all there is

could do such a thing.

God has the power.

He is Lord.

He has ordained the universe. From the tiniest atomic particle to the most massive nebula in the farthest reaches of space, he has spoken them into existence.

The most incredible thing about God is that even though all he has created is beyond comprehension, he is still instantly and constantly aware of the state and condition of each minuscule component. Nothing is unnoticed by him.

He knows the number of hairs on your head.

He knows how many grains of sand cover the earth.

He knows the atomic structure of each particle of the universe.

And his thoughts toward you far outnumber them all!

Hallelujah! What love! What power! What a God we serve!

Knowing that God has all power and yet does not force me to love him

makes me love him all the more.

Knowing that he has infinite knowledge and yet still has time for me

makes me want to follow him farther still.

Knowing that he chose to die for me while I was still a sinner

makes me want to forsake my sin and seek him
with all my heart—with all my existence.

He has the power to love. He is the power of love. He is
Lord.

MEDITATION

- What areas of your life are you withholding from his
  lordship?
- How does knowing that this kind of power exists cause
  you to view your own existence?
- How does Jesus display his power in your life?
- Do you feel powerless over sin? How does one overcome sin? How does one give up their own power (or
  powerlessness) and give up to God?

"Even in their sleep . . ."
Psalm 127:2 NASB

Ask the Lord to let you see the many ways he has displayed his love for you in your own life. As you sleep, look for his handiwork and power as manifested in your own life and existence.

To be an instrument in the hands of Almighty God, to have him blow through me with the Breath of his Spirit, is an awesome thing.

My heart is steadfast, O God;
I will sing and make music with all my soul.

Psalm 108:1

Maker of Music

The goal of instrumentalists is to become so "one" with their instruments that their instruments simply become an extension of their hearts.

When I sit at the piano, I want to be so confident in what I know about that instrument that I can pour myself out upon its keys and hear my heart played in an audible way. I want to be so in tune with the subtle intricacies of this specific instrument that every beat of my heart and every emotional rise and fall of my soul flow directly from the depths of my being through the black and white keys and into musical sounds. I want to be so comfortable (no matter my level of expertise) that it is difficult to tell where the keyboard ends and my heart begins.

I have the attitude that this instrument does not control me, but that I control it. My desire for control is born out of my desire to bless others. When I communicate my heart through music, I have the ability to convey memorable portions of my heart and feelings in tangible and audible ways that lift the spirits of others. That is my view of the one who plays the instrument.

But what if my heart and life were an instrument in the hands of God? Would he be able to express his heart and feelings for others through me, or would I resist his touch?

If I were a piano, I would need to tend to the wounds in my life and keep my life in tune with God's.

Some keyboards harden and grow brittle over the years through lack of care. When this happens, cracks often develop in the sounding board and the sound that comes forth, though possibly in tune, will be distorted by the buzzing and rattling produced by the brokenness of that sounding board.

The same holds true for our lives. When we do not properly care for the wounds and failures of our lives by laying them at the feet of Jesus, we tend to become hardened and bitter, harboring years of hurt. When the Lord tries to play his song through us, we may respond, but that response is hindered by the buzzing and rattling of that old hardness. Repairing a sounding board is virtually impossible—at best, patchwork may muffle the cracks and the hardness somewhat, but they are still there. With our hearts, though, repair is always possible through the grace and forgiveness we find in the love of our Lord Jesus Christ.

A piano may have a resonant and flawless sounding board yet still not be in tune. Strings (like the gifts God gives each of us to "sound" forth his presence to others) can become old and brittle if not kept in tune. There is a worldwide standard for tuning any instrument that enables instruments of many sorts and designs and functions to come together and play the same music. They may play from different perspectives, but they are still in tune with the concert master—the conductor. But if those strings are left alone and fall out of tune, the instrument—though beautiful on the outside—becomes an audible distraction. The musician may play all the right notes, but the uncared for strings distract from the very purpose they were intended to fulfill.

The wise musician takes the first flat sound as a warning that help is needed. He subsequently takes the proper steps to renew that flat-pitched string to its proper place of soundness and integrity. Our hearts can be like those strings. If we could take each wounding or failure and see it as a warning sign that something is out of order, if we could quickly contact the Master Tuner, Jesus, and ask him to bring us back to order, if we could be restored day by day, our lives could be veritable symphonies of praise!

To fall flat is not the end of the world. To lie there and do nothing about it is a shame—especially when the Master Musician freely offers the gift of repentance. If the Body of Christ could learn to play to the same standard of tuning— the Lordship of Jesus Christ—and disregard all the various, unimportant differences, we would free one another to enjoy the uniqueness of God's orchestra!

*If I were an instrument of percussion—like a drum or triangle—*I would find that the beauty of my existence is found in my response to the beatings of life!

A triangle is made of a metal that has gone through the purification process of intense heat. When that process is completed, the triangle—when struck—produces a pleasing sound, regardless of how hard or often it is struck. Like the triangle, we must see the fires of life as stretching and purifying factors that lead to the pleasing sounds of grace and holiness. Our sounds of grace and holiness lead others to the source of that sound—and ultimately to the Maker of Music.

My desire for control of my instrument is born out of my desire to bless others.

The drum, too, finds its beauty—its identity—in its response to the poundings of life. The drum produces a sound of majestic beauty that declares the unmistakable creativity of the Maker of Music—no matter how often or how hard the beatings come. Such "woundings" produce a melodic and rhythmic aroma that rises to God's heart and serves as a beacon of hope to all who hear it.

But a drum sounds distorted and overbearing when the striking surface is too loose or too rigid. When too loose, there is a lack of clarity. This looseness comes when the drum head is not stretched or tuned properly, producing an indiscernible rhythmic center. A lack of clarity leads nowhere. The other instruments have difficulty finding the beat when the drum cannot be heard clearly. Our hearts, like a drum head, become distorted and lead nowhere when we do not allow the Lord to stretch and tune us properly so we can offer to him a surface that is attuned to his rhythm.

If I were a wind instrument, I would have to learn to allow the Spirit of God to blow through me.

Since breath must be blown through wind instruments and across the reeds to produce sound, it is essential that the airways be kept free and clear. To be an instrument in the hands of Almighty God, to have him blow through me with the breath of his Spirit, is an awesome thing.

If I were a stringed instrument—like a violin or guitar—I would learn to bend my strings at the Master's bidding.

Such bending might seem painful or uncomfortable for awhile, but the song, when played by God, always sounds like peace and produces a melody of joy. At times, the Master may ask us to sound forth music that may seem violent or hurtful. As he plays a loud song of warfare or a bold song of deliverance through our lives, our heartstrings may be required to endure long passages of the greatest magnitude. Strings that are hard and brittle break under such heavy demands. But strings that bend and vibrate sympathetically to the Master's touch produce life, joy, peace, and endurance—a melody of love.

My desire is that my heart be a ready and in-tune instrument in the hands of my God. This is simply a matter of *relationship.*

He is the player.

I am the instrument.

He is the potter.

I am the clay.

What is so incredibly awesome about God playing in my life is that he sings *over* me as he plays *through* me (Zeph. 3:17). His song is the greatest love song ever written. Its melody is amazing grace and its chorus is redeeming love. Its harmonic structure is the joy of his embrace.

Play, Lord.

Play your song in me and through me.

Sing over me and hold me.

I am yours and you are mine.

MEDITATION

- What kind of instrument would you be in God's hands?
- Are you in tune right now?
- Are there any hard places in the sounding board of your heart?
- What melody would the world hear coming from your heart right now if they could audibly hear your heart?

"Even in their sleep . . ."
Psalm 127:2 NASB

Ask the Lord to let you hear his song as he sings over you through the night.

EIGHT

I will praise you

I Will Praise You

All that I am, all I will be,
All that I know,
And all that I cannot see,
All that I was is no longer me,
For my Redeemer,
My Lord, set me free!
He rescued me!

I will praise you
For all that you have done for me!
I will praise you
For redeeming and setting me free!
For loving me!

I was so lost and you seemed so far,
But redeeming blood washed me to right where you are!
Now I am your child,
And you are my God!
Your redeeming love
Just leaves me standing in awe
Of who you are!

INSPIRATION

Psalm 89:5–8; Luke 17:15–16
August 14, 1996

The enemy of God often tries to drag me down through deception—through lies. This song was born when I was feeling depressed and really had no reason (at least that I could see) to be so down. Most generally, the enemy attacks my identity and worth.

When those lies came, I simply reminded my soul of the truth: Yes, at one point I was unworthy and a sinful wretch, but the redeeming blood of Jesus cleansed me and made me righteous by his righteousness. Yes, at one point in my life I was hopelessly lost, but the Good Shepherd searched for me, found me, and rescued my life. I remembered how lost I was and how much Jesus had to pay for me, and my heart was filled with an awesome awareness of his mighty loving presence.

When I began to focus on these truths rather than on the enemy's lies, gratitude began to fill my heart. As I released the gratitude to Christ, the enemy was forced to flee from the presence of my Redeemer, and this song was born in the process.

I simply began doing what I know to do—I approached my Father in gratitude for all he has done.

He who has been forgiven much, loves much . . . I love you so much, Lord.

The light of the truth
shined into the dark,
hidden places of my heart.

When [the devil] lies, he speaks his native language,
for he is a liar and the father of lies.
John 8:44

Liar! Liar! What's the Truth?

The enemy of God is a deceitful liar! At one point he had me so convinced of a perverted identity that I could not tell the truth from a lie—ever!

Just as we take on the nature of our Father God when we are in Christ, so it is when we are dead in our sin—we take on the nature and character of the enemy. Thus, I became a liar at an early age.

Mind you, I would never lie about tangible things. If I ever took something that didn't belong to me, I could not stand the guilt—I had to confess! Why? Because being accepted was important to me, and I knew that people wouldn't like me if they thought I was a thief . . . and because it made me somehow believe I was really a good person because I did the right thing. What a joke! I was living two separate lives, even as a little boy.

On the surface, I was the talented, well-mannered one who made the honor roll and played the piano. Beneath was the hidden me . . . the me who believed no one loved him . . . who was overcome with the perverted need for male attention . . . who fell into homosexual behavior . . . who despised himself and wanted to die.

I had convinced myself that my behavior was normal. Though I knew deep inside that something was wrong with that picture, I had learned to lie even to myself. My day of reckoning came, though, when I could no longer hide the truth. My sins, as all sins tend to do, betrayed me! When I was "found out" and confronted, the light of the truth, as light tends to do, shined into the dark, hidden places of my heart, and I was forced to look at myself in the light.

When I saw the truth of God's love and the forgiveness, hope, and healing that he offered me, I allowed the Lord to pick me up and begin the healing process. As he raised me up from the grave where my sins were buried, he began to slowly loose the graveclothes that still bound me—and the lies and the personal beliefs I had toward myself began to give way to the truth and the beliefs Father God held for me, his child.

When the enemy reminds me of who I used to be,
the Lord graciously reminds me of who I am.
When the enemy reminds me of the experiential
knowledge I gained while in sin,

the Lord reminds me that I now have his mind
and that my past knowledge was washed
away under the blood of Christ.

When the enemy tries to cause fear and doubt about
my future,

the Lord's presence fills me with hope, and my
heart responds to him with trust.

When the enemy reminds me of how shameful and
vile my past was,

I respond to the Lord with gratitude and joy
for my redemption.

When the enemy tries to make me falter in my faith
by tightening some of those graveclothes I
still drag around,

I respond with the truth that this dead man
now walks in total freedom!

Truth is the only weapon against the lies of the enemy. To
discover the truth about what God thinks of us, we need go
only as far as his written Word. In many ways, God's Word is
like a love letter. And just as a love letter makes us want to
know the one who sent it, God's Word leads us toward relationship with him. Hear the truth of God's love letter to you,
and use that truth to overcome the lies of the enemy.

I am his child. God is my Father, and I can expect to be loved
and nurtured by him (1 John 3:1)! That truth alone took me
light-years ahead of where I ever thought I would be. When I
put on that truth, I was transported into the arms of a Father I
had always thought was distant and far too busy for me.

I belong to him. He chose me! I could not pay the debt I owed because of my sin, so he purchased me by the blood of Jesus (Acts 20:28). If I belong to him, there is nothing anyone can do to harm me. I may suffer, even die physically, but the true reality is that I belong to him (Rom. 8)!

I am a new creation. I am brand new (1 Cor. 5:7). All I used to be was crucified, buried, and left in the grave. Someone brand new rose up with Jesus! Me!

I am royalty, called to rule and reign with Christ (1 Pet. 2:9). I need to see my place in this life as a position of the highest purpose and calling, as a king who would lay down his life for his subjects. People need the Lord, and I know the way. There is no higher calling than to lead others to know him.

I am a priest. I no longer have to go through a priest to meet with God. I, as a priest, can approach God through my High Priest, Jesus Christ. I now have direct access to God through Christ (1 Pet. 2:9; Heb. 4:14–16).

I am an overcomer (Rev. 12:11). Just as Christ overcame sin, death, and hell for me, I can now face life knowing, with full assurance, that there is nothing I cannot do through him and his strength.

I am a warrior. We will stand (Eph. 6)! Christ has provided us with the armor necessary to face life and to battle the enemy—the father of lies. We need not be overcome by his deceptions. We need not live in fear of "what if." We follow the Captain of the Hosts, the Commander in Chief, the Lord Jesus Christ who has already won the victory for us!

I am accepted in the beloved. I used to think I had to perform for the approval and acceptance of God and others. I thought that as long as I jumped through all the right hoops, people would love me. After awhile, I grew tired of all that jumping and finally decided to jump off that track and into the acceptance and approval of my Redeemer. I do not have to perform for his love—ever again (Eph. 1:6)!

I am a servant of God. The heart and joy of Christ was to serve me by laying down his life (Matt. 25:21). Because I am in him, that is also my heart and my joy, as I seek to lead others to know and worship him.

I am loved. I was worth his life even though I was worthy of death (John 3:16; Rom. 5:8). Who can explain God's ways? I was unworthy, yet he thought I was worth giving up the riches of heaven for! I was worth his life. He is worth mine!

God delights in me. I believe he takes more delight in me than I could possibly take in him! He is God! He is able! He thinks of me constantly (Ps. 139). I cannot do that toward him, yet that truly is my desire. In fact, he is able to think that way about each and every individual. Amazing!

These are the truths that set us free!

Wouldn't you like to know the sender of this love letter a little more intimately? Then put off the lies and receive the truth about all he thinks concerning you! You are precious and wanted! He delights in knowing you . . . and desires that you delight in knowing him.

MEDITATION

- How would you describe who you are?
- How would that description be altered if God's enemy were giving it?

- How would that description be altered if God were giving it?
- What lies do you need to put off right now?
- What truths do you need to put on right now?

"Even in their sleep . . ."
Psalm 127:2 NASB

Ask the Lord to continue revealing lies to you and then to help you receive the truth—even while you sleep.

When runners
fall, they get right
back up, set their
eyes on the goal,
and run toward it
as if their lives
depended on it!

Do not gloat over me, my enemy!
Though I have fallen, I will rise.
Though I sit in darkness,
the Lord will be my light.

Micah 7:8

⁂

Will I
Praise You?

Relationship is based on a mutual covenant—an agreement between two hearts to exchange life.

I was in need of God, so God stepped in with life— exchanging mine for his. God was "in need" of a broken vessel to pour himself through, and by his grace, he allowed me to be such a vessel. He gave me life, and now I am honored to give it back to him.

Because my mind had been entrenched in so many lies concerning my identity for so many years, the enemy of God often reminds me of all that I was, and he tries to convince me that, inherently, nothing has changed. Of course, nothing could be further from the truth! But from time to time, I stumble in my thoughts: "Maybe I am kidding myself. Maybe I really am a failure . . . maybe I am less than a man." But the beauty of a relationship from God's perspective is that it is based on the truth of a mutual covenant. I do not plan to fall, but if I do, God will still love me—and he will be there to set my feet right back on the path. *That* is the truth!

When running a race (which is what the Christian life is like), runners do not go back to the starting line if they fall. No, they get right back up, set their eyes on the goal, and run toward it as if their lives depended on it! That is a picture of repentance.

And my life *is* dependent on the Lord! I fall. I see my need for a Savior. I turn to him. I run to him for help! That kind of relationship—that kind of love—fills me with gratitude, because I realize that, except by the grace and love of God, I would surely be defeated.

Praise becomes a springboard into the deeper places of relationship with Almighty God.

When failure comes or when the enemy assails, we have a choice to make: Will we allow that failure to define who we

200

are, or will we lay claim to who Jesus has defined us to be? Will we allow the voice of the enemy to shout us down, or will we outshout his clamorous lies with praises to our God and Savior? I have chosen the Lord, and he has chosen me! By his blood, I was signed, sealed, and delivered—lock, stock, and barrel—and there is no one who can take that away from me! When confronted with our own weakness or by the lies of the enemy, the question becomes very simple: Will I praise the Lord in the midst of it, or will I allow the relationship to be breached by my lack of communication with the Father?

When I first set out on my journey to know God (way back in 1981), I had just graduated from college with a degree in church music. Needless to say, the only job I could find was that of a school bus driver. But I soon realized that God had engineered my circumstances to allow me to get to know him. Since I didn't know where to begin, I simply sat at the piano each day, between my morning and afternoon routes, and sang my heart out to Father.

At first, all I knew to do was place my Bible on the piano, opened to the psalms of David, and cry out David's words in song to Jesus. What I found myself doing, more often than not, was simply thanking God for all he had done in my life.

As I look back on those times, I now understand that I was simply taking my first baby steps. Much as a toddler, who is first learning to walk toward the outstretched arms of his daddy, I was moving toward my heavenly Father! The truth is this: I simply began to praise him through the expression of gratitude, and, through that expression, found spiritual legs. I no longer had to crawl but could walk—and, finally run—toward the Father.

So, what exactly is praise? Most dictionaries define *praise* as "admiration, appreciation, or commendation." I like the way Webster defines it: "admiration or gratitude expressed." Gratitude, or gratefulness, is simply being appreciative of the benefits one has received. As I sang through the psalms day after day, I discovered that whenever words of praise were used by David, they were almost always in the context of gratitude, extolling the ways God had benefited his life.

In other words, praise is simply giving thanks to God for who he is and for what he has done! *Gratitude expressed becomes praise.* Psalm 107:1–2 (one of my "life" passages) reads: "Give thanks to the Lord, for he is good; his love endures forever. Let the redeemed of the Lord say this—those he redeemed from the hand of the foe." Expressing our gratitude also takes the form of declaring, or telling others, what God has done: "Come and listen, all you who fear God; let me tell you what he has done for me" (Ps. 66:16).

Having been set free from the sin of homosexuality in 1981, gratitude was frequently on my mind. I had a ready affinity with Paul, the "chief of all sinners," who said: "I thank Christ Jesus our Lord, who has given me strength, that he considered me faithful, appointing me to his service. Even though I was once a blasphemer and a persecutor and a violent man, I was shown mercy" (1 Tim. 1:12–13).

Praise becomes a springboard into the deeper places of relationship with Almighty God. Gratitude should be the attitude of every worshiper. Yet, the simple truth is that even a nonbeliever can express gratitude to God for something he has done. One can believe in God yet not know him. In other words, praise does not necessarily require *relationship*.

I have seen people, void of a life-changing relationship with God, receive something (like healing or financial help) and readily thank God for what he had done—only to go right back to the ungodly life they had lived prior to God's intervention. We have all seen movies in which the "hero" is lost at sea or in some dire situation. At some point, he says, "God, if you get me out of this, I'll change my ways."

Of course, the hero always makes it, and he "thanks" God verbally—but nothing else changes. Did he praise God? Yes. Did he have a relationship with him? No—one can praise God and not know him. But, I believe, one cannot *worship* God without a true knowledge of him—without a "knowing" relationship.

Believers, we have been given the joy of walking in relationship with the God of the universe. To allow anything—calamity, lies, heartache, or trials—to come between the Lord and our hearts is to cut off our very lives! We must face this life determined to cultivate and nurture that *exchange of life*. One of the best ways to keep those channels open is simply to . . .

remind yourself of all you have been forgiven,

climb up on that springboard of gratitude,

jump as high as you can,

then plunge deep into the center of God's heart.

Will you praise him? How can you not?

MEDITATION

• What do you have to be thankful for?

- What are some of the lies the enemy constantly confronts you with?

- How are lies best put down?

- What truths about yourself does God desire you to walk in?

- Why is praise so vital in our relationship with God?

"Even in their sleep . . ."
Psalm 127:2 NASB

As you prepare for sleep tonight, ask the Lord to remind you of all the reasons you have to praise him—then praise him as you lie down! See if you don't wake up with peace on your mind!

Those who give up
to the wave are swept from
the island, washed from their
pitiful existences, and freed to live
with and be loved by the King.

*But the Scripture declares that the whole world
is a prisoner of sin, so that what was promised,
being given through faith in Jesus Christ,
might be given to those who believe.*

Galatians 3:22

I Was So Lost

Are there degrees of lostness? I really don't think so. Lost is lost! Perhaps our notion of degrees of lostness is merely misperception.

When I was a little boy, I remember being in a large department store. As little children will do, I wandered away from my mother. She noticed that I was gone and began searching for me frantically. She found me quickly, as I was only one aisle away, and was overjoyed to discover her lost boy. I had been lost, then found—yet through it all, I was totally oblivious to the danger of my situation.

One of my favorite television shows, while growing up, was Gilligan's Isle. You know the story: ship lost at sea . . . Gilligan . . . the skipper too . . . the millionaire and his wife

. . . the movie star . . . the professor and Mary Ann—all stranded on a deserted island. If anyone was lost, they were! I used to picture myself on that island with them. They were always devising crazy ways to signal help, yet always missing hope by brief seconds as rescue somehow always eluded them. They were hopelessly lost, and they (along with millions of viewers) knew it!

Who was the most lost—me, who had no idea that I was lost, or the folks on Gilligan's Island, who were aware of their desperate situation every minute of their lives? In reality, I was just as helplessly lost as the Skipper's crew. That little lost boy was as close to disaster as the nearest child abductor, as the nearest door out onto the nearest busy street. He was just as near hopelessness as the crew of the S. S. Minnow on Gilligan's Isle.

Our relationship with God really does boil down to how we perceive our lostness prior to our entrance into that relationship. I have known many who lived morally good and noneventful lives right up to the point of their salvation. I have heard some of them express their disdain toward those who lived lives of hellions, and I've seen them respond to God with a lack of gratitude—much like the ones who tried to keep the prostitute from washing the feet of Jesus. These men were reprimanded by his acceptance of the social outcast they despised. The one who realized her lostness and need of a Savior was the one who gained relationship with Christ. Is it any different for believers today? How lost do we have to be before we realize how much we have been rescued from?

The picture I have in my heart is of a slave encampment on a distant island, guarded by the evil enemy of God. The inhabitants of the island are in bondage to the enemy and spend their days walking around in hopeless despair. At the center of the island lies a deep volcano where all the captives will one day be cast—should they not be rescued.

Some of the prisoners are held only by a small leash. Since they are no threat to the daily routine of the enemy, they are left virtually alone, except for that leash. Sure, the leash is an inconvenience, but it is not a great detriment to their lives. They scarcely realize they are being held captive and have long forgotten the doom that awaits them if they are not rescued.

Others on the island are very much aware of their captivity. They carry such heavy burdens that they are unable to breathe at times. Heavy chains are their only covering. They are constantly beaten down by their captors and are covered with deep wounds. They are consigned to living out their existence in a miry field of clay where few survive. They are pitiful and disgusting—and they know it. The heartbreak of all this misery is that those on the leash mock those who carry the heavy burdens. Both are hopelessly bound—but only the ones with the heavy chains realize it.

One day, a mighty rumble is heard on the island. At first, the prisoners believe it is the dreaded volcano. Yet, as they look out to sea, they are confronted with the sight of an oncoming tidal wave. That wave is ridden by a King who seems to be its very driving force. Towering over the inhabitants, it crashes upon the shore and covers the entire island. The chains of all the prisoners are loosed, and those who give up to the wave are swept from the island and washed from their pitiful existences to the land of the King—freed to live with and be loved by him.

That island was my bondage. The wave that swept over me was the love and blood of Jesus, sweeping me far away from my bondage and captors and releasing me in the kingdom of light. I realized how lost I had been—just as lost as the most bound—just as lost as the least bound—just lost. If we could all see how lost we really are apart from Jesus, the Body of Christ would be full of dynamic servants who readily pour out their lives to see others swept away by the love that swept over them. We were freely given love. The love we have received is to be freely given away. He who has been forgiven much, loves much, and gives much. Those who do not understand the depth of their lostness do not.

I am in no way saying that my sin gave me some sort of advantage. To the contrary! I wish I could say I had not walked in such depravity. How I wish I could say that! But I cannot. My heart's desire—and I believe the Father's—is that all believers recognize the depth of their redemption and then walk accordingly.

I was so lost, and you seemed so far.
But your redeeming blood, Lord, washed me to
right where you are!
Now I am your child, and you are my God!
Your redeeming love just leaves me standing in awe
Of who you are!

MEDITATION

- How lost were you?

- What would your life be without the salvation offered by Christ?
- Where were you on the island of lostness?
- What do you have to be thankful for?

"Even in their sleep . . ."

Psalm 127:2 NASB

Ask the Lord to show you your life before you knew him. Ask him to fill your heart with gratitude.

I have come to see
that he is as near
as I will allow
him to be.

Now we see but a poor reflection as in a mirror;
then we shall see face to face.
Now I know in part; then shall
I know fully, even as I am fully known.
1 Corinthians 13:12

To Know Him

Worship has to do with *knowing God.*

Quite literally, the word *worship* means "to acknowledge the worth of something." But how do we acknowledge the true worth of someone unless we get to know that person? And how can we know the *Creator of the universe* in an intimate way?

I used to think of God as a cosmic policeman who was only interested in me when I messed up. In my mind, when I sinned, he would zoom into my life, zap me with some punishment, then zoom out again to resume his distant and controlling stance over me (much like the "church police," or pharisees, of our day).

But I have come to see that he is not distant at all, but that he is as near as I allow him to be. It is his desire to be intimately involved in my life. If I allow him to come into my life, he continuously interacts with me—he speaks to me as I speak to him.

I sing to him . . .
> He sings to me.

I dance before him . . .
> He dances with me.

I bow . . .
> He cleanses.

I fall . . .
> He picks up.

I sin . . .
> He redeems.

I seek to know who I am . . .
> He gives me my identity.

Do you get the picture? We get to know God as he interacts intimately in our lives. But allowing God to interact in our lives requires that we *trust* him: "Trust in the Lord with all your heart and lean not on your own understanding; in all your ways acknowledge him, and he will make your paths straight" (Prov. 3:5–6). In other words, if I will seek to know him, with and through every aspect of my life, he will direct my paths.

As God began to reveal his true nature to me, he also began to reveal my true identity. One of the ways he taught me of himself was through the different meanings of his many names. Since God's names and their meanings helped me understand him a little better, I naturally became curious as to the meaning of my own name. I was somewhat disheartened, though, upon learning that the name Dennis was actually a derivative of the name of the Greek god of wine, Dionysus, who celebrated the power and fertility of nature. (I think I got the fertility part down!) Literally translated, my name meant "follower of the Greek god of wine"! I had hoped—and even expected—that God would reveal some deep, never-heard-before apocalyptical revelation of my destiny and identity. Instead, I was relegated to be associated with mythology!

Yet, God in his mercy and grace (not to mention, his patient and kind sense of humor), knew I would not be satisfied with that meaning. As always, he is a Redeemer. And as he did with my very life and being, he also would do with the name used to identify me as me.

As I sat there sadly wondering why God would give me such a name, he reminded me of his covenant with Abraham and Sarah—and how he had changed their names. In so doing, he had actually changed what they knew of themselves. Their name changes called them to a deeper understanding of his will and of their identities, and along with these changes, he placed his seal of commitment and approval on their lives. He had done the same thing with Jacob (whom he named Isaac) and with Saul (whom he named Paul). If he could change their names and identities, why couldn't he change mine?

Guess what? He did! When we are born again, we become brand new creations—God gives us new identities. If we have new identities, it is our desire, I believe, as children of God, to know not only who he is but to find out who we are as well.

Before, my name meant "follower of the god of wine."

Now, God has given a new meaning to my name.

Before, I had worshiped a false God.

Now, I worship the true God.

Before, I was bound in sorrow.

Now, I am free to rejoice in my God and his liberating power.

So, now, whenever I hear my name, it serves to remind me of who I am—Dennis: a happy, rejoicing follower and worshiper of the one true God!

I admit, there are days when I find it difficult to hear God and to know him in an intimate way. But isn't the recognition and confession of that need the first step in a relationship?

Paul, too, struggled with his limitations in knowing God. To the church in Corinth, he confessed that he did not know God as fully as he desired and that, at times, he could see God only dimly (1 Cor. 13:12).

My desire to know myself can only be adequately met in knowing my Maker.

MEDITATION

- Do you know God to the depths that you desire?

- Do you think you know all you need to know of him?

- What hindrances to knowing God do you sense in your own life?

- What would it take to overcome those hindrances?

- What are some questions about yourself you need answers from God concerning?

"Even in their sleep . . ."

Psalm 127:2 NASB

Ask God to take you on a spiritual journey of discovery as you sleep. The destination? The meaning of your name as it reveals your new nature in Christ.

The creation always
reflects the heart of the
one who created it!

Ascribe to the Lord the glory due his name;
worship the Lord in the splendor of his holiness.
Psalm 29:2

Face to Face

I believe that worship is living in a *face-to-face relationship* with God through Jesus Christ by the power of the Holy Spirit.

The foundation of such a relationship is understanding that I desperately need him and that without him I would be hopelessly lost. I need him more than I need the air I breathe—I need him to sustain and maintain my very existence—I even need him (not gravity) to hold me to this earth.

Who made the gravity?

Who made the air I breathe?

Who gave me life?

Who overcame my homosexuality?

Who bore my sin on the Cross?

219

I can do nothing for myself. I certainly could not save myself. Only one could do that—Jesus Christ. The truth is that I need him to meet every need of my life—and ultimately, he does!

I believe that all people, if honest with themselves, feel an emptiness—a void—deep inside that compels them to know their purpose for existence and to know the someone greater than themselves who is responsible for their existence. God is Creator. We are the creation. The creation always reflects the heart of the one who created it! If our Creator loves us, then isn't our heart's deepest desire to love him? Isn't the heartcry of all mankind to know God?

> For by him all things were created: things in heaven and on earth, visible and invisible, whether thrones or powers or rulers or authorities; all things were created by him and for him. He is before all things, and in him all things hold together. (Col. 1:16–17)

> You are worthy, Our Lord and God, to receive glory and honor and power, for you created all things, and by your will they were created. (Rev. 4:11)

When I recognize my desperate need, my response is to seek a face-to-face relationship with him in worship. But how do I "flesh out" such a relationship?

Worship begins with *trust*. Trust means presenting our hearts to God and saying, "Lord, here I am. I cannot see you clearly, for the dust of this life has settled on the glass of my heart and I see you only faintly. Would you please take me to yourself and wipe off that dust so that I might see you and know you a little better?" Worship is trusting God enough to let him take your heart and cleanse it—free it—of anything that separates you from him.

Worship continues with *honesty*. I remember the first time I was honest with anyone about my struggles. After the initial "revelation," I ran away; but eventually, I came back to face the music of rejection. But instead of rejection, I was met with a chorus of grace and acceptance and the words, "I believe God can heal you; and whatever it takes for you to be healed, I will walk through it with you!"

I remember feeling so clean and light, as if the weight of the world had been finally lifted from my shoulders—because it *had* been lifted from my shoulders! When I finally accepted that same love from Jesus, I was swept away by his deep and jealous love. It was that kind of love that enabled me to be honest. It was that kind of honesty and truth that set me free. It was that kind of freedom that made me desire a face-to-face relationship with God—I desired that relationship so much that I was willing to forsake whatever I needed to forsake to find it! Honesty is the basis of my relationship with Christ. Even when I don't hear his voice or understand his ways as I would like—even then—I can be honest with God and trust that he will not "write me off" or consider me a hopeless case!

At a practical level, worship is simply *obedience* to God. Obedience requires surrender of our wills to the truth of his will. Giving up my will does not mean a loss of personal identity, as we see in the practice of many cults. Obedience, and our subsequent surrender, follows our recognition of our complete need of him.

Worship is also a matter of *choice*. It's true that God's Word *commands* us to praise him and worship him, yet God does not force us to love him. The beauty of any relationship that bears fruit and life is that it is entered into of and by one's own choice. God chose me. And he allows me the freedom to choose him in return. Yet, because of the holiness of God, we know that one day every knee will bow and every tongue will confess that he is Lord. That is reality simply because he is God. But God never forces us to *love* him.

So why do we have verses that command us to love and worship him? I believe it is because he provided the law (his commandments) as a teacher that guides us to the truth. Ultimately we need God, and we need to know him. Like parents who command their children to do their homework because they know they will need that knowledge to succeed in corporate life, so, too, Father blessed us with his law because he knew we would need to know him if we were to truly succeed at life! He commanded us: "Love the Lord your God with all your heart and with all your soul and with all your strength" (Deut. 6:5; see also Mark 12:30).

At a practical level, worship is simply *obedience* to God.

Further, worship is an act of *confession* and, therefore, healing. "Confess your sins to each other and pray for each other so that you may be healed. The prayer of a righteous man is powerful and effective" (James 5:16).

How does confession bring healing? If I went to a physician seeking healing for a certain ailment but would not tell him where I hurt, how could I be healed? Confession is not for the doctor but for the patient! Yes, God knows where we hurt, but do we trust God (the Great Physician) enough to allow ourselves to be vulnerable to his healing? Sin is the ultimate ailment. When the "cells" of our heart have been rid of the "germs" of sin by the "antibiotics" of redeeming blood, life is no longer hampered and the flow of relationship is once again restored—and healing of the soul takes place.

Do you see how confession is simply one more facet of worship? If we desire a healthy relationship with our Creator, then, as with our physical bodies, we must feed our souls with the proper diet: a diet of relationship through confession, praise, and worship.

Finally, worship is *drawing others to Christ*—and this, too, has to do with confession—confession of our faith in Christ. When Christ is lifted up, he draws others to himself (John 12:32). As I praise God publicly through my testimony of redemption, as I share the intimacy I have come to know with my God—he uses me to draw others to see that their deepest needs can be met through knowing him, just as mine were.

Our outward life is merely a reflection of our inward life—who we really are (or at least who we think we are!). If we do not outwardly confess Christ, aren't we really denying him? "Whosoever therefore shall confess me before men, him will

I confess also before my Father which is in heaven. But whosoever shall deny me before men, him will I also deny before my Father which is in heaven" (Matt. 10:32–33 KJV).

"Praise the Lord! For it is good to sing praises to our God; For it is pleasant and praise is becoming" (Ps. 147:1 NASB). In other words, praise looks good on you. Praise does a body and soul good! If praise does that, worship—the depth of relationship—will do the same . . . and more!

To know God is to live a life of worship before him. To know God is to walk in relationship with him—especially when the days grow dark and the walk becomes wearisome.

Knowing God leads to life.

MEDITATION

- What are some questions about God you would like him to answer?
- What will you do if you do not receive the answers you are looking for?
- What will you do if you receive no answer at all?
- What does trust in God mean to you now?

"Even in their sleep . . ."

Psalm 127:2 NASB

Ask the Lord one specific question before you go to sleep. Trust him no matter what you hear!

shout to
the Lord

Shout to the Lord

Shout to the Lord if the Lord has saved you!
Shout to the Lord if he knows your name!
Shout to the Lord if the Lord is Savior!
Shout to the Lord if you will never be the same!
Shout to the Lord who is King now reigning!
Shout to the Lord if the Lord is King!
Shout to the Lord who is King, proclaiming!
Shout to the Lord who reigns over everything!

He is—my Redeemer! He is—Lord of All!
He is—Salvation! He is—Lord of All!
He is—my Shepherd! He is—Lord of All!
He is—my Healer! He is—Lord of All!
He is—all Glorious! He is—Lord of All!
He is—Victorious! He is—Lord of All!
He is—Almighty! He is—Almighty!
Jesus Christ is Lord of all! So . . .

Shout to the Lord if the Lord has saved you!
Shout to the Lord if he knows your name!
Shout to the Lord if the Lord is Savior!
Shout to the Lord if you will never be the same!
Shout to the Lord crucified, forgiving!
Shout to the Lord for the life he gave!
Shout to the one who is risen, reigning!
Shout to the Rock, to the one who alone can save!

He is—Lamb of God! He is—Lord of All!
He is—King of Kings! He is—Lord of All!
He is—Everlasting! He is—Lord of All!
He is—More Faithful! He is—Lord of All!
He is—Worthy! Worthy! He is—Lord of All!
He is—Holy! Holy! He is—Lord of All!
He is—Almighty! He is—Almighty!
Jesus Christ is Lord of all!

INSPIRATION

Psalm 66; Matthew 21:8–9
December 31, 1995

"Shout to the Lord" came to me on New Year's Eve, 1995. Each month we have a Night of Praise in Oklahoma City. This time of worship is one of the highlights of every month for me. Each New Year's Eve, we ring in the new year by worshiping through the midnight hour and into the first day of the new year.

As I prepared for the celebration that day, God gave this song as an affirmation of who he is and of who we are in him. For me, this song is a personal thank you to the Lord for the awesome year of blessing he gave me and my family in 1995—in spite of all the trials and heartache (and time spent in recovery for Melinda!).

I taught the song that night and was overwhelmed by the response of the people. May God bless you and affirm you as you exalt him with these words!

I am on the team
of the King who has
already won the victory.

My lips will shout for joy when I sing praise to you—
I, whom you have redeemed.

Psalm 71:23

Shout to the Lord

Some things are worth shouting about.

Certain circumstances evoke strong emotional responses—even from ordinarily meek people. I am not talking about the normal responses we have to sorrow—like weeping—nor am I speaking of the hearty chuckle one expects to follow a good joke well told.

I'm talking about the meek and mild-mannered gentleman who becomes a raving lunatic when his favorite running back from his favorite team scores that tie-breaking touchdown!

I'm talking about that young mother of three who is normally soft-spoken and known for her grace, dignity, and charm who suddenly transforms into a foghorn when dinnertime approaches and her children have not returned from play with the neighborhood children!

I'm talking about the quiet and reserved little, old lady who is known for her gentle demeanor who suddenly begins to behave like a Dallas Cowboys cheerleader on Valium simply because she bingoed!

I am talking about the man who seemed a hopeless case to everyone around him—as well as to himself—who suddenly realizes his lostness and receives hope and salvation from Christ and cannot help but leap for joy amidst shouts of "Hallelujah!"

I am talking about the Father God who has been waiting so patiently for that prodigal son to return, who, upon that return, suddenly cries out for all the heavens to hear, "Rejoice! For that which was lost is found! The son whom I had lost has returned! Announce it to the ends of my kingdom! Start the music! Kill the fatted calf! Let the heavens rejoice and the earth be glad! My child has returned!"

I can see myself vividly in each one of these scenarios. When you win at something, it is difficult not to rejoice about it. When Braveheart won the Academy Award for picture of the year, I shouted! When my son hit that first home run, I jumped up and rejoiced for him! When my team wins the pickup basketball game, I rub it in to the "enemy" boisterously and unashamedly! When I get Mario past the first level of Nintendo (or when I simply keep from falling off the path and into the great abyss of Nintendo), you would think I had won the lottery! I love to win! And when I win, I feel I must respond accordingly.

Even when at a movie, I feel I must invest emotionally in the action. (I figure since I paid six dollars, I bought the right to be part of that movie!) While watching the Kevin Costner version of Robin Hood a few years ago, my true emotional colors were quite evident. By the time the drama had unfolded to the point of that final confrontation between good and evil, I was cheering Robin on! When the witch unexpectedly lunged out of the shadows, pointing a sword toward the hero, I jumped and shouted, "Look out, Robin!" Most in the theater laughed out loud (they had really wanted to do the same thing); my only detractor was the gentleman behind us who said, "That guy needs to be theater trained." Oh, well.

Being raised in a noncharismatic church setting, I was not accustomed to the level of outward expression demonstrated at my Grandmother Jernigan's church. I grew up feeling an obligation (because of my traditions) to downplay that type of emotion—even ridicule it—even though I really liked the way it made me feel sometimes.

But in other settings, I was one of the loudest voices. At ball games I rooted loudly and passionately for the lowly underclassmen. After all, it was my duty to cheer on the ones who would follow in the rich heritage I would one day leave them—due to my prowess on the basketball court, of course (you may gag yourself now!). I could get worked up emotionally when it came to the things I considered important.

But all that changed. As I grew physically, my bondage to sin grew as well. By the time I ended my college career, I honestly felt I had nothing to shout about. I considered myself a failure.

I felt worthless.

I felt unnecessary.

I felt vile, dirty, and unworthy.

I felt like a nobody.

I believed life would be better for others if I was not around.

I had a depressed heart.

I often wonder why the response of that woman who anointed the feet of Jesus so bothered the disciples. (The same guys who didn't want the children to get too close to Jesus). With costly perfume she bathed his holy feet and, with a heart overflowing with gratitude, wiped them dry with her hair. This whole display threatened the disciples' own need for approval based upon their performance.

They still didn't understand all that was to take place through the death and resurrection of Christ. They had no concept of new birth, as Jesus would reveal it. They had no concept of the once-and-for-all sacrifice Jesus was about to become. I think they were also bothered by the emotional display of this woman. Much as a child, jealous for the attention of a parent, tends to put down the sibling who seems to easily and readily receive the attention they crave—so the disciples felt compelled to put down another in order to feel better about themselves.

When I think of how they must have felt after Jesus' redeeming work was accomplished and they began to retrace such memories in their minds and hearts, I think they must have quickly and deeply learned the proverbial truth that "laughter does good like a medicine"! In my heart, I believe the woman probably left that solemn and serious gathering and hit the streets *shouting!*

Think about it. Quite often, the healing touch of Jesus evoked a very emotional response from the touch-ees! Shouting and leaping were the method of the day. Even Jesus himself got in on the leaping and shouting action. When the disciples returned from the mission he had sent them on, boasting in the power of God to work miracles and cast out demons, Jesus rejoiced and boasted in and to the Father (Luke 10:21 NASB). ("Rejoice," in this instance, meant literally to jump up and down for joy.)

When King David danced for joy at the return of the Ark of the Covenant (the representation of God's presence), his wife, Michal, was disgusted. I wonder why. Was it because he danced? Dancing was an integral part of their culture. Was it because he danced so scantily clad? He was king. How dare he degrade himself that way! But is that what his subjects saw? Or did they see an example of gratitude, a foreshadowing of the New Testament teaching that "he who has been forgiven much, loves much"?

When I realized my own redemption, I could not contain myself at times. Even when I would release a shout of joy, it somehow never seemed enough for the one who had set me free!

> I had felt there was no hope for me,
>> yet Jesus saved me!
> I had felt like a nobody,
>> yet Jesus knew me and called me by name!
> I had felt alone and hopelessly bound,
>> yet I was now befriended by a Savior!

I had felt like such a loser,

> yet now I was on the team of the King who had already won the victory. (I read the end of the book. We win.)

I am now a servant of the King and Lord of all!

> Never again will I allow my joy over a touchdown to be more rowdy than the joy I have for my Savior.

> Never again will I respond to those who worship with exuberant shouts as I did toward the people my grandmother worshiped with.

I will join them.

> Never again will I be like the disciples and try to dissuade or discourage others from responding enthusiastically like little children to the Lord.

I will join them.

> Never again will I degrade or defile the joyful release of love by redeemed ones to the Father— however exuberantly expressed (as long as they keep their clothes on!).

I will join them.

There is a time to be silent before the Lord, and there is a time to respond to that winning slam dunk. Jesus won my freedom! That is all the slam dunk I need.

MEDITATION

- Does outward expression of worship bother you? Why or why not?

- What are some things you get excited about? Why?

- Why is our understanding of how lost we were so important?

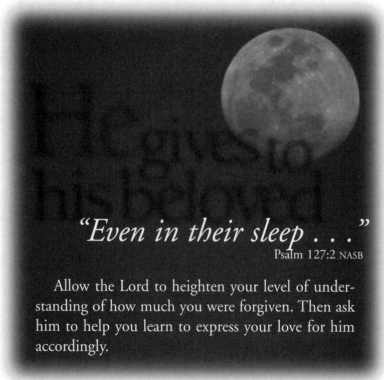

"Even in their sleep . . ."
Psalm 127:2 NASB

Allow the Lord to heighten your level of understanding of how much you were forgiven. Then ask him to help you learn to express your love for him accordingly.

We must remember that—even when we momentarily stumble or fall—we are on the winning team.

Shout for joy to the Lord, all the earth,
burst into jubilant song with music.
Psalm 98:4

Something to Shout About

There really are a lot of things to shout about.

When I was a child and would cry or whine for no reason except self-pity, my parents would often say, "Stop that, or I'll give you something to cry about!" Well, for all who are being overrun by the lies of the enemy—and those lies often reach shouting levels—I say, "Stop listening to him. I'll give you something to shout about!"

I have found, being the father of nine very expressive children, that to be heard, I often have to increase my volume to a sizable decibel range in order to override the din in the Jernigan home. It is no different with the enemy! He is a liar, and he lies often; and even though his lies are frequently subtle, he leaves us feeling shouted down! But we must remember that—even when we momentarily stumble or fall—we are on the winning team. We serve the Victor! We win!

When the clamor of the lies grows louder, our resistance to the lies must grow even louder. In other words, our intensity in proclaiming the truth must match and surpass the intensity of the enemy's lies. We need to be reminded that we really do have something to shout about!

Here are some things to help us shout him down:

I was a nameless prodigal.
He called me by name and welcomed me home.
He is Lord of all!

I was bound.
He set me free.
He is Lord of all!

I was lost.
Jesus saved me.
And he is Lord of all!

I had gone astray like a sheep.
He led me to safety and shelter.
He is Lord of all!

I was wounded in my sin.
He healed me.
He is Lord of all!

I was clothed in graveclothes and self-righteousness.

He clothed me in his righteousness and surrounded me with his glory.
He is Lord of all!

I was on the losing side of life.
He won the victory for me.
He is Lord of All!

I was weak.
He became my strength.
He is Lord of all!

I was a slave to a false King.
He made me his own and now reigns in my life.
He is Lord of all!

I had no means to pay my sin debt.
He became the Lamb crucified for my sin; he paid my debt and washed me clean.
And he is Lord of all!

I was dead in sin.
He gave me life.
He is Lord of all!

I was buried under a mountain of sin.
He raised me up.
He is Lord of all!

My life was built on sinking sand and was swept into a raging sea of despair.
He became my foundation and planted me firmly on a solid rock.
And he is Lord of all!

I saw no future for myself.
He gave me an eternal destiny.
He is Lord of all!

I could trust no one.
He became one I could trust. He is faithful and
true.
And he is Lord of all!

I was worthless.
He gave me worth from the depths of his own
worthiness.
And he is Lord of all!

I was dirty and insignificant.
He washed me and set me apart for himself.
And he is Lord of all!

When in doubt about what is true or right, I simply remind myself of what King David did when his own men wanted to stone him. Upon returning to camp after battle, he found the women and children taken captive; and then his own army turned on him. What was David's response? God's Word tells us that he encouraged himself in the Lord (1 Sam. 30:6). We must learn to do the same.

One of the simplest ways to overcome the enemy is to have a plan of counterattack—to be ready for his deceitful assaults upon your identity before they come. Note: if you are in Christ—if you are born again—the attacks will come. If they do not, something may be wrong!

How do we remain ready? By constantly putting on the truth. The simplest way I personally apply the truth is by remembering three basic commands of Christ:

1. *Love God.* Does what I am hearing cause me to doubt God in some way or cause me to be hindered in my relationship with him? This may be a lie!

2. *Love yourself.* How can we convey the love of Christ to others if we have not received it ourselves? Does what I am hearing cause me to respond out of my identity in Christ? If not, it is a lie!

3. *Love your neighbor as yourself.* Does what I am hearing cause me to respond in love toward those around me? If not, I am hearing a lie!

This may seem overly simplistic to you, but in reality, it never hurts to be reminded of these fundamental truths. These three small axioms really do engulf every area of our lives, since life is about relationships and how we respond in each of those relationships. Lies, like dust on a window, cloud even the best of relationships. And like windows, the dust of our lives need periodic washing with the water of the Word of God's truth.

Above all else, Christ is Lord. He rules no matter what. One day, every knee will bow and every tongue will confess, even those who are on the enemy's—I mean, the loser's—team. When in doubt, listen for the voice of the Lord and head for the Cross. His voice is the goal post, giving us guidance and direction, and the Cross is the scoreboard, declaring the truth that the game really is over—and that we really do win!

I don't know about you, but that kind of makes me want to shout!

MEDITATION

- What do you personally have to shout about?

- What are some lies that the enemy shouts into your life?
- What truths can you use to put them down?

"Even in their sleep . . ."
Psalm 127:2 NASB

Ask the Spirit of God to reveal lies you have believed and then reveal to you the truths you need to put them down.

he will reign forever and ever

He Will Reign
Forever and Ever

Who overcomes the darkness?
Who shelters me in storms of life?
Who alone is the Helper of helpless?
Who reigns in love with pow'r and might?
Who is the King of Glory?
Who is the reigning Lord of Life?
Who alone is Light in the darkness?
None but my Lord Jesus Christ!

He will reign forever and ever!
Lamb crucified, Risen Savior, and the Lord of Life!
He will reign forever and ever!
King of Kings and my Lord, Jesus Christ!

Who makes a way in the desert?
Who puts the enemy to flight!
Who fills me with peace in confusion?
Who gives me grace through the long, hard night?
Who is the Hope in hard times?
Who is Comfort when we don't understand why?
Who alone can bring life from dying?
None but my Lord, Jesus Christ!

Who is the one who will never leave us?
Who is the Savior Crucified?
Who is the one who died for sin
And rose again to give us life?
Oh! Oh! Oh! Oh! Jesus is his name!
Oh! Oh! Oh! Oh! Jesus Christ will reign!

Who is the King of Kings and
Lord of Lords in my heart glorified?
Who is the one overcoming hell,
Redeeming me with brand new life?
Oh! Oh! Oh! Oh! Jesus is his name!
Oh! Oh! Oh! Oh! Jesus Christ will reign!

INSPIRATION

Exodus 15:18; Revelation 1:17–18
February 21, 1996 and February 24, 1996

This song began being born in my heart during the last week of February of 1996 as I was being oppressed by the enemy and confusion seemed to be all around me. During the days between when the song was begun and when it was finished, a terrible accident took place in nearby Muskogee.

A mother and two sons were involved in an accident with a freight train. The mother and six-year-old were killed. One son lived and another had stayed home that day. One minute the family was there, and then the next, half of them were gone. Several families in our church were affected by this tragedy. God showed me at that time that this song was for our body and for that family as a reminder that God is still in control—even when (especially when) we don't understand why such terrible things have to happen.

May the words and boldness of the music cause you to rise up and bless God as the one who reigns through any tragedy, through any trial. He is the Giver of Life, even in death, and he rules and reigns over it all—forever.

With God,

the joy truly

is in the

journey.

May the God of hope fill you with all joy
and peace as you trust in him,
so that you may overflow with hope
by the power of the Holy Spirit.
Romans 15:13

Joy in the Journey

Life is full of heartache.

Many people simply give up on living or are so overcome with the hardships of life that they don't seem to care about themselves or anyone else. For some, the heartache seems almost nonstop.

I recently heard the story of a young man whose father had died when he was a small toddler. He was one of six children, whom his mother now had to care for alone. Only a few short months later, his mother died, leaving the young children no alternative but to live with an aunt who was already supporting five children of her own—alone. Yet she took in her nephew and nieces and raised them as her own (eleven children in all!)—not only caring for their basic needs of food and shelter, but also making sure they had a solid spiritual foundation.

Each child was even given the opportunity to further his or her education, and with his acceptance to a major university, this young man was able to attain a seemingly unattainable goal. When asked what she attributed the success of her family to, this loving aunt confidently said, "It was the Lord. We chose to focus not on what we did not have—but upon what we did have."

Upon hearing this story, I was touched in a deep place in my heart. Here was a woman, with an insurmountable mountain of responsibility, yet her faith in God said that her mountain was indeed movable. In fact, it was obvious that she had not feared the mountain; rather, she had enjoyed the journey.

When others saw sheer cliffs,

> she saw the faithfulness of God.

When others saw insurmountable mountains,

> she saw the ingredients for building deep and lasting character in the lives of her young charges.

When others grew weary and gave up,

> she found the strength to carry on.

When others were blinded by the clouds found in high places,

> she set her sights beyond the clouds to the vista that awaited her at the pinnacle of the struggle.

Yes, at times, the only view she had was of the ground staring up at her, but even the ground held its own special glimpses of God's presence—of his majesty. When the way grew slippery, she saw little signs of God's provision supporting her and lifting her, even though each step was a major, pain-filled effort—an education in suffering. Most would have seen the logs as roadblocks to progress; she saw them as footholds from the Lord. She was thankful for what she had—not bitter because of what she didn't have. She saw God's majesty even in the hardships of life.

If all we see in the journey of this life are the bumps in the road,

> we may miss the whole point of living.

If we are overly concerned with the length of the journey,

> we may miss the very joy life was intended to bring.

If we do not follow the leadership of the Lord,

> we may find ourselves stranded on a deserted back road, complaining and confused as to where we should go and ultimately going nowhere.

If we allow the little distractions of the journey—the flat tires, the overheated engine, the detours— to consume our minds and our strength,

> we will end up settling for the scraps of life rather than feasting on the riches of the table God has set before each of us.

Of course, road hazards are real and must be dealt with, but they should never deter us or cause us to turn our eyes or our hearts away from the focus of our destination. I would hate to think my life could be so consumed with worry over the little bumps in the road that, because I kept my eyes downward so much of the time, I missed the grandeur of all life has to offer along the way!

I must admit, however, that at times I am more concerned with my outward appearance—with keeping my car polished and shiny—than with following the path God has set before me. And still, at other times, I allow my fear of the journey to cause me to sit stranded at a standstill—doing nothing, yet keeping that outer car looking spiffy! What a boring life!

What is more important to God, the condition of the outer shell or the tuning and condition of the engine? What is more important to the Lord, that I get to the destination looking good but having seen nothing of life, or that I follow him on both the superhighways and the off-road endurance races that life can bring? Give me a journey through the back country any day!

With every pothole,

> I'll be looking for the beauty of the forests that stand watch over me on either side.

With every flat tire,

> I'll be enjoying the satisfaction of a job well done and the opportunities to thank God for his provision.

With every roadblock,

> I'll be waiting for the hand of God to make itself
> known to me in some unexpected way.

With every stranded motorist I encounter along
the way,

> I'll see countless opportunities to express the
> boundless love of the God who created it all.

From the roughest, lowest valley road, I will choose to see the foreboding mountains as beacons of hope rather than insurpassable obstacles. When I come to a flooded river that appears impassable, I will see yet another opportunity for God's great power and creativity to be made known in my life. When I cross the deserts of dryness, I will be refreshed in knowing that the coolness of his Spirit awaits me at some point along the way.

How can we enjoy and appreciate the cool, refreshing rain,

> if we never experience the long and weary heat
> of the desert?

How can we enjoy the healing power of God,

> if we never experience the woundings of this
> life?

How can we ever know the full extent of joy,

> unless we face the sorrows life will bring?

How can we know the depths of life,

> if we never experience the hopelessness of death?

How can we fully appreciate the sweet presence of
God,

if we never experience times when he seems far
away?

How can we be comforted by the Light,

if we have never cowered in fear at the darkness
of night?

With God, the joy truly is in the journey. We can either
focus on what we do not have, or we can feast upon all we do
have. Remember, in the hands of God, even two small fish and
five small loaves of bread can become a feast to five thousand!

The majesty of God is where you find it. Don't be so
focused on the hazards of life that you miss the little points
of interest along the way. Where is the majesty? Just look
around . . . and you'll find joy in the journey.

MEDITATION

- What are some of the road hazards you face?
- What are some of the evidences of God's majesty you
  have missed because of focusing upon those hazards?
- What brings you joy? How can you know joy in the
  midst of sorrow?

"Even in their sleep . . ."
Psalm 127:2 NASB

Ask the Holy Spirit to take you on a journey as you sleep. Allow him to reveal some of the mysteries of God's majesty you may have been missing.

Behind the storms of life—even
in their midst—we find the
majesty of God.

He stilled the storm to a whisper;
the waves of the sea were hushed. . . .
Let them give thanks to the Lord for his unfailing love
and his wonderful deeds for men.
Psalm 107:29, 31

The Majesty

What demonstrates God's power more—the countless, invisible mysteries of the microscopic world or the vast unsearchable expanses of a gigantic universe? What provides more evidence of his power—the ability of a small microbe to defeat a ravaging, life-threatening infection in a child's blood stream or the ability of his voice to speak the atomic power of a star into existence?

To me, the greatest demonstration of God's power is his power to *change a life*. The power of love transcends all other displays of power combined. The fact that he chooses to live his life in and through me—in relationship with me—is the most awesome evidence of his power of all. And I believe all those other demonstrations of his power exist simply because he loves us.

When I first realized that homosexuality had a grip on me, I felt so alone—as if I were in some dark and concealed room where there was no light. I longed for the light—instinctively knew I needed the light—and I knew, somehow, that the light would help me. I just didn't know how to get to that light. I couldn't produce it myself. Any light I could have produced would have been only temporary, leaving me even more helpless than before.

The light finally appeared to me—and it was the light of Christ. The light found me. I did not find the light. I had tried to meet my own needs in so many ways that I could not tell the darkness from the light. It took the soul-rending, heart-searching light of Jesus Christ to reveal my desperate state.

But, hallelujah! Once that light was revealed, my heart suddenly had direction. Not only could I see that the darkness of the room had been shattered by the light, I saw that the light of Christ had carved a way out of my dark existence—but I had to follow.

Beyond the darkest night of life—

even in the midst of the most dreadfully dark times—

we find the majestic light of God.

Tornado Alley, where we live, was recently assaulted by a rash of springtime funnels. Immediately, my children knew what to do. As soon as I got the word "tornado" out of my mouth, my children were already in the cellar. The darkness of that shelter represented life and hope and safety to them.

Though it was by no means a comfortable place for our large family (and the family of five that had just dropped by for a visit!), we were at peace because we knew our shelter was strong and secure.

This reminded me of the tornadoes I had endured as a child on this same farm and of how we had experienced them all without the shelter of a cellar! As a child, storm season was my most fearful time of year—no place to run, no place to hide. All we could do was wait it out and hope for mercy! Even though we were never physically harmed by these storms, the emotional woundings left their mark for years.

To feel the difference, now, after all these years, was something of a revelation for me. In sin, I had been like a ship on a stormy sea, totally at the mercy of the waves of deception and temptation, carried away wherever they would lead me. But when Christ intervened, I felt safe from the storm, just like my children felt safe in that storm cellar. I had come into a place where nothing could touch me—a place where peace and safety were the atmosphere, even though all manner of evil flew about me.

Behind the storms of life—

even in their midst—

we find the majesty of God.

Melinda and I make a conscious effort to teach our children to be responsible for their actions and attitudes. One of the ways we try to instill wisdom in their lives is to give them certain responsibilities on the farm. They get to see firsthand what happens to a little baby chick if it is not taken care of—

and their sense of compassion for others is enhanced in the process. If they do not close all the gates after feeding the horses, the horses are apt to find that opening and head for the highway—and certain danger. In the process, the children learn that there are reasons for rules and reasons we are so protective of their lives.

From time to time, though, I have to watch my children encounter tasks they cannot complete. Sometimes, the physical strength needed is simply not there yet. Sometimes, the zero-degree weather makes it unbearable for a six-year-old to water her pigs, or for a seven-year-old to feed the goats, or for any of the children to break the ice on the watering trough so the horses can drink.

Sometimes, as I watch them—trying to complete their chores in inclement weather or struggling to get that bale of hay to the hay rack—I see them come face to face with their own weakness. It is during those times that I intervene and help them in their helplessness. Usually, they are grateful, but there are times when—trying to prove themselves—they tell me they don't need my help, or they struggle against me in their effort to be seen as capable and self-sufficient.

With God, it is no different. We must face our helplessness and accept his help. Otherwise, we will struggle against loads that will crush us. But to accept his help is to walk in true strength of character. To accept his help is to gain yet another insight into the magnitude of his majesty.

Behind my weaknesses—
    even because of them and through them—
I find his majesty.

My best friend has a child who was born with a rare and life-threatening disease. My friend and his wife are faced with constant uncertainties as to her future and their need for a miracle. For years, they have sought God's healing power—believing he is totally capable, yet never seeing that healing in a physical sense. What they have discovered is that, even though this infirmity is a real and constant presence, God's grace is more sufficient to sustain them than this sickness is sufficient to defeat them or their little one.

Why do bad things happen to good people? Why do good things happen to evil, sinful people? Why does God allow suffering and heartache in the lives of his children?

First, he is God, and he has all the answers.
>Seeking him for answers is a good way to get to know him.

Second, where sin or evil abounds,
>grace abounds much greater! Hallelujah!

Third, as with my own children,
>it is in facing the heartaches of life that we grow in our ability to know and trust God.

Without the pain of the wounding, how would we know the joy of the healing process? I don't understand it all. I just know it's true. God's majesty is displayed through his grace. Every time we cry out to him for help, he is there with more grace. Even when questions are left unanswered or even when death knocks at the door, his grace is more than sufficient; and with that grace comes yet another opportunity to grow in relationship with the Giver of Grace—Jesus Christ.

Majesty is where you find it.

Majesty is the grace of God lived out through my
own heart.

Majesty is the relationship I am able to enjoy
with the Creator of all that is.

Majesty is knowing Jesus Christ.

Majesty is a King who will reign through the storms,
shine through the darkness,
comfort in the sorrows,
strengthen through our weaknesses.

Majesty is God reigning in me—
truly a mystery!

MEDITATION

- What is the greatest revelation of God's majesty in your life?
- Have there been any instances in your life where it was difficult to see God's majestic touch? How did you respond?
- In what specific ways would you like to see the majesty of God declared in and through your life?

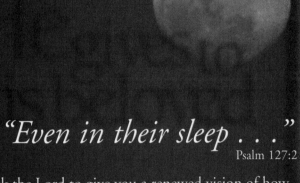

"Even in their sleep . . ."

Psalm 127:2

Ask the Lord to give you a renewed vision of how he might declare his glory and majesty through your life, so that when you wake there will be no doubt about who he is and whose you are!